The Call

Leah N. Edwards

Copyright © 2026 Leah N. Edwards

All rights reserved.

ISBN: 979-8-9944414-0-4

DEDICATION

To my mom, the Grammar Queen, who has bestowed her grammatically correct gifts and organizational intellect upon me. To my family who has shared the journey...and to you, who honors that this is my point of view and my family may not share these perspectives nor be open to conversation about this. Thank you for respecting their privacy.

This book was written, channeled, proofread over a dozen times (including applying the healing techniques each time), edited, and illustrated by me with 0% AI assistance.

Preface

Why am I writing this book? Writing this book requires a ton of vulnerability. After a lifetime up to this point of not being seen or heard clearly, I'm getting that now is the time to address Energetic Awareness. When you have a pattern of people misunderstanding you over and over, no matter which group you're in, even if you move, it's a common response from people that, *"...you're the common denominator so you must be the problem."* But I'm not a poor communicator. What's also true is that if you're the common denominator, maybe you are the difference that life has been asking for to shed awareness about a new phenomenon, or maybe not new, but something that has been going on that no one has addressed on a larger scale. People have become more aware of energy and have deeper questions in life, wanting to find out why things happen the way they do and how to prevent what we don't like in order to improve our quality of life.

I've found that you can't get very far unless you start looking at energetic awareness. I write from the perspective of watching the energy flow from people's intentions... and based on the energy that they are, noticing outcomes that match the energy of the person. In no way, shape or form am I here to silently observe scenarios and then "scarlet letter" everyone for their faults in a tone of blame. The problem with society is our urge to jump to conclusions, assume and judge which does not leave room for energetic awareness. If an example I use sounds familiar, my aim is to use as few identifying descriptors as possible so that no one is personally exposed and embarrassed about their situation.

When we have more energetic awareness, we can see what really created the results that are showing up so that people can be seen clearly instead of black-balled erroneously. In short, we need to grow a little. Energy doesn't lie. If you're reading the energy, then you know what's actually going on and you can live from a higher space of consciousness. This book is a calling for us to expand our consciousness and abandon the ways that hurt ourselves and each other. We can't act like those who came before because that was a different time. We need to create better versions of ourselves so humanity can stop reinforcing methods that have long ago expired and that create more issues.

Will *you* answer The Call?

Table of Contents
Part 1

Dedication

Preface

1	Community: IRL vs. Online	Pg # 1
2	Align & Agree, Resist & React	Pg # 5
3	Cognitive Dissonance to Truth	Pg # 9
4	Coming Together Within	Pg # 13
5	Yearning For More	Pg # 16
6	Playing the Game	Pg # 20
7	An Early Call	Pg # 23
8	Breaking the Frequency	Pg # 25
9	Recognizing The Call	Pg # 32
10	Answering The Call	Pg # 37
11	Putting the Kind in Humankind	Pg # 43
12	Clarifying Intentions	Pg # 47

Table of Contents
Part 2

13	Start Where You Are & Work Watcha Got	Pg # 52
14	You Can't Get There From There	Pg # 59
15	Hindsight is 20/20... Foresight is 20/15	Pg # 65
16	When We Know Better, We Do Better	Pg # 68
17	Enough is Enough	Pg # 71
18	Be the Change You Wish to See	Pg # 74
19	Follow Through & Circle Back	Pg # 78
20	Environmental Impact	Pg # 83
21	The Whole of the Piece that I AM is a Piece of the Whole That We Are	Pg # 86
	Affiliate Link	Pg # 89
	Music Link	Pg # 90

Part 1

1
COMMUNITY: IRL VS. ONLINE

We're living in a time when even the youngest adults have grown up on social media. They don't know a time when we weren't online. People are a mixed bag of being wired the natural way of face-to-face conversations, calling people, mailing them, engaging in proper social protocols like eye-contact, smiling at and holding to door open for strangers, saying pleasantries as you pass them in addition to adapting to newer ways of communicating like emailing, texting, video chatting, and creating online profiles. Although convenient and necessary in today's fast-paced world, technology-based communities are a synthetic form of community that involves training ourselves to be accustomed to screens in lieu of human eye-contact, seeing flat images lit up instead of 3D people, places and things IRL (in real life) with their own energies, aromas, mannerisms and energetic information that the auras carry. Online communities are necessary for building online business...I'm not negating its role in today's culture. But a world of information is missing online that is perceived and received in person, in real life.

Some of us know the challenges in dating apps these days where the person can look and sound good all day long by uploading their best pictures, spin the best narratives, but then when you meet them in person, their voice doesn't turn you on, their personal smell stinks-and I don't mean an odor...I just mean there's no chemistry from their natural essence. If you've been trying the dating app world without reviewing the results that you've been getting and applying the experience, then you might be trying to make it work because their profile is on point. While the analytical mind wants to say, *"Oh, but we put all this time into our chat. We got to know each other first."*, this is simply the mind overriding your intuitive sense which is feeling that- *This is not a match. This is not working out.* This is why I have hung up dating apps...people have not been seeing the logic of- *"OK matching doesn't mean we're in* an online relationship...It means we need to meet in person ASAP to see if we vibe with each other in real life...we can have great conversations in a chat all day long, but it doesn't mean anything compared to your senses of smell, sight, touch, energy exchange- being in their presence." I have no desire to dive into anonymous chats before meeting in person. True, some of their essences can transfer through the digital world... I've read people's pictures intuitively by seeing them, but a lot of times, what's lost in translation can only be experienced in person. It's also noteworthy that we tend to fill in the gaps in our minds, projecting the version of a partner onto them that we're hoping they are while we're in an online chat versus being open to receive who they are while we're in person. This creates a false version of them that only exists in your mind then when you do meet them in person, you have two different identities to merge as one and what has happened for me is they're nowhere near who I thought they were. So, then you're starting all over once you do meet in person. It's just a big time suck to dive into a penpal chat situation without meeting in person first. So we're missing a whole lot of information by solely being online and maybe you didn't realize that *the digital dating world wasn't working* and that *this is why*. But we are multi-sensory beings and we need to have all our senses available and experienced.

    Sometimes I forget what time I'm living in as I walk into a spiritual center on Sundays...I expect to see the age ranges of all people represented as it was 20 years ago. But in reality, what people have gotten accustomed to is fast-paced life, PJ culture (wearing pajamas or leisure-wear 24/7), and being anonymous while watching/streaming from home. Most profiles don't require you to have a real picture of yourself, let alone a recent picture of yourself so many people hide behind their favorite pic or hobby or sunset instead of a face, their identity. As I walk into a spiritual center these days, it's more like most people are over the age of 60. And then there's me and maybe one other person under the age of 40. I really wish this wasn't the case and I don't like bringing it up because it kind of feels like I'm chopping down what little attendance spiritual centers have these days and they're thankful for their online community. I'm also thankful to be able to stream services and things online when I can't get out either...things come up. But I still crave that physical experience in my life. I bring this in because many of you are missing from that physical experience.

    When I started teaching workshops years ago, I was looking forward to having my own Louise L. Hay or Wayne Dyer career and building over time, seeing attendance rise and building a following- not out of ego, but out of living my purpose helping people, out of inspiring people to align within and find out what their soul is here to do and be since I fully feel that everyone has a purpose and unique spiritual gifts to bring forward and discover excitedly how we can use these to enhance our lives. But I guess I started teaching around the time that physical attendance had begun waning and I thought, *"What is going on?"* It took a moment but then I realized disappointedly, *"Ohh...people are trending online."*- it was the rise of influencers. People were starting to make money on YouTube by monetization. And who wouldn't? Who wouldn't want an easier way to generate income and be able to travel the world or achieve goals? But I don't think that this replaces in-person, in-real-life community.

When you're in person, you get to shake hands with people, hold hands and feel the group energy in the room as you sing the departing song when the event closes...you get to hug people you just met, but also feel that soul energy as if you've always known them. You get to smell a variety of personal smells. I don't like saying the word smell here... maybe aroma is a better word. Everyone has their own natural aroma, their soul scent...it doesn't have to do with hygiene, it's just who they are.

Being physically in a community, you get to hear people's voices... how unique they are and undistorted by technology, as some people sound a little more nasal through the lens of technology but in person they are a completely different sound. I guess every solution creates another problem. It's two sides of a coin. I'm thankful for online communities and the ability to build business wherever you are in the palm of your hand, but I charge the younger people and also other people who have adapted and steered heavily into the technology world at any age - When's the last time you put your phone away while out in public, sitting at a cafe or a bar? When's the last time you struck up conversation with wait staff? A passerby? When's the last time you practiced active listening with a stranger? At one point the question came to me, *"Why hasn't anyone tried to get to know me?"* And then it occurred to me, *"Oh, they stalked my social media's past posts and thought that was enough. That sucks."* Spying is not the same thing as connecting with them.

My grandpa used to "never meet a stranger" as they would say. He would get into a conversation with someone after picking up food and I'd be waiting forever for him to come out saying, *"Where do you know them from?"* He was like, *"I don't, we just got to talking..."* and it would have been a 40-minute conversation. Having conversations and unexpected interactions brings value to someone's life. It makes a human that you don't even know feel like they belong and that things are going to get better, even if they don't know how, and even if they didn't even talk about their problem. It's a human connection that they didn't have before and it's irreplaceable. It also feels great for yourself too, so it's not about just the other person. The breakdown in communication happens with conveniences like- instead of people replying a true heartfelt statement online, just clicking the "like" button on something. While that generates responses and interaction to some degree, it's absolutely the bare minimum somebody could do to be in conversation with you. While it's convenient to "like" so much, What's asking to be shared and contributed in a conversation? Can we settle in a little deeper in our state of presence and ask- If this is the last conversation I ever have with this person, would I still just "like" their comment or would I actually engage with them? What can I be and do to bring value to this space?

2
ALIGN & AGREE, RESIST & REACT

Whenever I start a new practice, I like to think about the most challenging places that those practices are needed in order to sharpen my skills. Yes, that would be what a high achiever does and this is what I do for myself. I'm constantly being my own life coach, challenging myself to reach greater heights and putting myself in uncomfortable situations. This is what motivators usually talk about...getting comfortable with being uncomfortable. However, most people don't do that and they don't think about doing it on purpose for themselves unless somebody challenges them to do so. I often have reminded people that there really is no competition. Your life journey is about you - Not in a selfish, entitled way like some influencers think that statement means. It's about you competing with you and you challenging yourself to grow even greater while also having your life mission centered around being an asset to your community...and if there is any comparison, we are comparing ourselves to our former versions of ourselves, offering our wisdom to other people who also wish to grow or to start growing faster. That's why we are helping each other, not because there's the one and only right way to do something or because some people are superior to others. It is simply the journey of the one having their experience and each one having their own experience and people having a yearning to try a different way to master life so we reach out to each other. That's what strengthens communities. We need connection because we need each other. And it's not up to other people to help us all the time or to constantly look outside ourselves to see who needs our help. But it's also a fact that we're not alone here, and we're naturally created and bent to look for community and look for a place to belong and to get strong. The problem shows up in community if people do not realize that their journey is a solo journey and they should be self-motivated rather than motivated by the outside. By this, I mean we shouldn't be constantly trying to fit in and blend in with other people and keep up with their pace that's unnatural for us. When you're motivated by the outside, then you fall into the slippery slope of "align & agree and resist & react". When you have aligned and agreed with a group of people on one topic, then you have to naturally resist and react to the opposite of that topic. If there are sinister forces on the planet who are trying to manipulate the masses so that they never are conscious and aware of what's actually going on, then they will use the "align & agree and resist & react" against everyone and put on this dramatic puppet show of pitting one community against another based on the belief systems that people are aligning with and resisting to. In other words, they seek to exploit feelings.

We can unpack the whole politics game here. I mean, politics or not, in general, people are looking to align and agree with something or resist and react to something. And due to politics every four years when campaign season comes around, there has been so much propaganda and energy pulled and pushed towards this versus that, I often don't hear back from people once they hear I have an opposing view about something. I'm generally not red nor blue, but I'm somewhere in the middle because I'm choosing consciousness. If you choose consciousness, you have to see the good and the bad about red and the good and the bad about blue. And you have to see how each side is using XY and Z against each other. Until we decide to choose consciousness fully over and over each time and rewire ourselves from being polarized out of our control for this and against that, we will not have freedom from the tyranny of politics pitting us against each other.

Each side knows what to say with a loophole that will hang people up to get mad about. One example that I can illustrate is the red will say, *"We are pro-life. We but we leave it up to the States."* Then a blue person will say, *"Oh my God, they're against abortion"*, but they're not against abortion- they leave it up to the states. So why can that loophole of the states having the power to make their legislation and their rules be enough for the blue person? If they were in a non-abortion state, couldn't they just travel to one that does allow it if they ever needed it? **Or is it really not even about that?** Usually, it's not about the thing we're arguing about...It's the fact that our power has been pulled in and sucked into an argument on autopilot, and it's designed that way. These polarizing topics pull us in so that we don't have our power, and we can't think clearly because once your emotion is caught up into an argument, usually consciousness goes out the window. And this is as far as I'm going into politics. I just used one example. If you're willing to see the energetic scenario for what it is, then you can start untangling your power from politics and from that model of "align & agree and resist & react". But if you're not willing to see, you'll probably think you have the right to be mad at me. That's not what I'm here to do. I'm not on either side. I'm just thinking logically, which to me is consciousness. If a part of you is now angry at me wishing to rebuttal and get into a debate, then that's where your power is tangled up. **If you can't take in opposing viewpoints and consider them equally and neutrally, you don't have control over your choices and your energy flow. What I am referring to is the skillset of being in dominion over your energy flow, no matter what the topic is.**

If you want to be free, you have to be conscious, and in order to be conscious, you have to be neutral. If you think about where you have pitted your power on this topic versus that on whatever side, consider that maybe each opinion is an anchor point and you've anchored yourself down to that side. Wherever you've anchored yourself down, you've created a blind spot to something else. And it's in the blind spots where people try to get away with things. They slide things under the radar in those spots. If we are willing to see and surrender our ego enough to not have a point of view about something, remain neutral and expand wide enough to encompass all points of view and see the good and see the bad then no one can manipulate you...you can't be duped.

I learned from an early age that it's easy to pull the wool over people's eyes who are not willing to be conscious. I'm hoping we see the change of that in my generation because the more we are conscious, the more we get power over those who are making life so difficult. There's many solutions on the planet that don't create more problems but it requires an enlightened approach as far as how different life will be compared to how it is now. Some spiritual circles would want to call this "living heaven on earth". I've often heard some spiritual circles claiming we need to revert back to no one owning anything and the earth is inherently all of ours – humanity's. A sinister point of view is "owning nothing and be happy" but behind that, their real intent is that they own everything and they are the deciders of our fates who don't own anything. While "heaven on earth" and "own nothing and be happy" seem similar, you have to be willing to see the sinister agenda behind the blind spots. Everyone who proposes a good idea doesn't have a good agenda behind it. If we're not willing to see the secret agendas behind it and what they're actually for and against, that's where we get stuck. I'm not sitting here pointing my finger, blaming anyone. I'm sitting in a space of compassion and reverence to how simple things can be once we all start choosing

The Call

consciously. But everything is a habit or a pattern, so we have to also continually choose each moment to moment, and the more we do so over time, it becomes the new habit, a new pattern and the new way of being. So, it's totally possible. I see us there already. Will you join me in this vision?

3

Cognitive Dissonance to Truth

Why do people not want their beliefs challenged? Usually if they have aligned and agreed with something that isn't the most conscious, and it is pointed out to them, then they have to face whether they want to really be aligned with something false or more limited, keep on putting their head in the sand, digging their heels into a narrative that has no logical basis vs. feel differently (and typically an ego buster). It means being different. It is a frequency change. Some people are not willing to lose the control that they have in place where everything is normal and everything is miserably comfortable. What would life be like without XY and Z? If they've held a belief system for many decades, it can be jarring to see life in a different way. It is a dramatic change to shift consciousness to the opposite of your long-held beliefs and will require starting over with social circles in the new belief system. Some people aren't brave enough and they keep things the same even though it hasn't worked for them in a long time. If you ever do make a jarring change, it doesn't have to be painful. I mean the easiest way to make a change is to move away and start all over physically because there, no one knows you and knows who you were before, so you don't have to run into the same circles of people. But people do change drastically and stay in their hometown as well. If you do make drastic changes and continue to see the same people in your same town, the frustrating part is not everyone updates their version of you in their minds, and if you are energetically aware, you will feel their projections of old versions of you from their minds being projected onto you every time they see you. If you're able to deal with that over and over, kudos to you. I have changed scenes altogether because it is annoying to deal with. Some people have cognitive dissonance about the changes people have made in their lives…like how could someone change that much in a short span of time? But everyone doesn't change at the same pace and sometimes you've been desiring the transformation deep down that you told no one about and when it clicks, it clicks and you can be drastically different in an instant.

FACING COGNITIVE DISSONANCE:

It's alarming if you find yourself getting swept up in a trending movement based on a false narrative. It's jolting and jarring to find that:
1. You didn't realize it was happening,
2. Shock that that there's so many people on board with it, and
3. How do we get this far with no one else realizing that this is not right? It's kind of a three-point whammy to process. Depending on the person- how their mind is wired and what their life experience has been, cognitive dissonance might set in on the first question, not even the second or the third. Are you daring enough to unpack each question and evaluate? Where do your loyalties lie? Loyalties are the secret agendas underneath it all that often hold people together who are misaligned. It's kind of like the grout between the tiles. It is subtle intention made long ago and sometimes it was just energies already there when you met the person that seemed to magnetically keep you together. But when you start digging down and questioning your loyalties, how you truly believe, then you can get clear on everything. Do you think that your loyalties with your friend group fully support you? I think what you'll find is that when some of your loyalties shift, your manifestations will get clearer and show up for you individually faster. Some of our loyalties are like weights keeping us from soaring. Would you be willing to see?

I had to face it with religion years ago, but in one sense, I was always on the fence. What caused me to entertain parental belief systems was when you're threatened with physical discipline early on, i.e.: the belt, "The Law of the Household" has already been set. Violence is the way the elders chose to solve problems so either you go along with what they say, or you get to suffer physically for rebelling against it. The path of least resistance was to be a good girl or a good boy and do whatever your parents say and believe whatever they believe so you don't get beat and you don't have to feel the pain and the process of healing from that violence over time. It was a no-brainer why people gave their power away at such a young age to religion, especially if some of these demented minds think that discipline is physical to begin with. **Discipline is a mind process. It is not physically beating your child into submission and to the point where their willpower is severely challenged as an adult later.**

After being whipped into submission early on, it's like your mind is divided- *"OK, I'll play the role, I'll play the part. I'll see how far I need to go with it until I'm safe."* But when is it safe? When is it safe to challenge your own belief systems and think for yourself? Did we forget to circle back and adjust?

Even though I was raised in a Christian home, I was noticing that the law of attraction was very real and active throughout life. I would notice the patterns of people attracting things. And I would look at my own manifestations, wondering how I attracted something that I didn't really feel was true to me. I had to come to the weird realization of seeing that it was possible that other people's energies were getting stuck in my flow to the point where I'm attracting partners that my mom wants for me or my sibling wants for me or living in a location for other people. From there, it got to the point where I've questioned everything- have I ever received anything that I wanted because I wanted it or because other people wanted me to have it? When is the last time I have received something for me because I wanted it, it was 100% for me?

If you're willing to ask deeper questions, you can move through the cognitive dissonance about what's really creating your life, even though we weren't taught that life is a certain way...that these are real and valid experiences for us...what I'm referring to is the nature of energy and how other people's energies can impact our lives even though we didn't know it was happening. I will say the more you dig in and find out what's true for you, the more you are true to yourself. The more you are truly 100% You, the more the universe shows up for you. Better things start showing up for you, not just essentials and not lackluster manifestations. It may be physically nauseating to create your own path, to think differently than everyone you've ever known in your life for decades, but it may be necessary. At the end of the day, you have to ask yourself, whose life am I living anyway? What is all this for? What did I come here for? Is there more to life than this? While I'm not aiming to invoke an existential crisis here (we all know someone who can over-analyze questions to death)...what I *am* asking is, Are you open?

CLARITY OF TRUTH TECHNIQUE:

Set Your Intention: **"If there is a universal answer, Truth about Life that is real I didn't know before, I'm now open, ready and willing to receive it."** By setting the intention, I'm choosing to stay open, to see the signs of synchronicity reveal as they do, to hear confirmations and answers to questions that other people didn't know I asked, and to hear that small still inner voice (God's) even louder each time. Since I'm nurturing that that connection, I have community within myself, and the community within myself is between me and God.

I always used to say this when I went to religious churches growing up, that if God is omnipresent, God is also in you. Then people would leave perplexed. No minister was ever saying that and yet the dogma would say that we needed to invite Jesus into our hearts. Why? If the definition of omnipresent is everywhere present? If God is everywhere present, God is also in you, which means your Soul You. Everyone has a Soul and it is an expression or extension of that God Consciousness coming here to be born in you, through you for this experience...but it's not running the whole show since we also have Free Will. I've always noticed life to be a balance of Free Will and Divine Will which can also be called Divine Order.

I have these friends I met at an event once and after talking, we traced back our experiences to find that we would have met two other times before that. We were all at those events together but never met until the third event. This is a great example of Divine Order or a Divine Appointment. It was Divine Order that we crossed paths in this life at some point, and there were several opportunities to do so, but we finally met the third time we saw each other. We had the Free Will to introduce ourselves to each other at the first couple of events, but we didn't because certain conversations were had, decisions were made, and so it was the luck of the draw that we did not meet those first two times.

Ever since I noticed this balance of Free Will vs. Divine Order/Will, they have been the foundation for how I view life. Too much Free Will activated, and the ego is running amok (usually corporate world's issue – they are spiritually lawless and making grave mistakes). Too much heavily relying on *"Is this Divine Order/God's Will or not?"* and you're giving your power away, waiting for blatant magical signs when there's practical ones unfolding for you right in front of your eyes- like the story of one praying for help and the boat came by and the helicopter came by but they didn't notice all the times that they were almost rescued. There is a point of being too spiritual and over-existentializing signs, synchronicity and symbols (i.e., obsession with numbers to the point of pigeon-holing your point of view). We're here for a physical experience as well as spiritual, so we need to balance the two and know when to zoom in and when to zoom out. Keep in mind- Is this Ant's Eye View or Eagle's Eye View?

4

COMING TOGETHER WITHIN

If we're not doing "align & agree and resist & react" and we really are in that space of consciousness, open to collaborate, hear others' differing points of view, and still find common ground with them, then what keeps us apart? Sometimes wounds and the fear of wounds being retraumatized keeps us from wanting to come back together with either those who hurt us or just the idea of immersing in another community or group of people where you could be hurt again. Every case is different. There are periods where staying away and finding solitude are absolutely necessary in order to stop being retraumatized over and over again. There is a gray area for each person and everyone heals in a different way. You can't say, *"Oh, I'm in this stage so I'm OK to go out"* because just like grief has stages, and healing is cyclical, so is trauma. I will add this caveat here though, that modern medicine usually does not acknowledge- **It's not** *"once traumatized, always traumatized,"* or *"once a diagnosis always a diagnosis"*. **Yes, there is a healing journey, but also, there is the possibility and reality that the healing work is done. Miracles do happen, full healings do occur, and if you find the right modality and/or the right combination of modalities then you absolutely can unhook yourself where traumatic things and situations hung you up inside before.** People loop because part of them is still going back to that scene, to the scene of the crime basically, and they didn't get seen or heard or something they saw or heard was so out of this world they could not feel whole about it and did not know how to process it. There have been many developments over the years between traditional medicines you ingest or energywork experiences that have been on the planet for thousands of years, like acupuncture, that go a long way to restoring a person or as I would like to say, *"factory-resetting a person before the point of injury"*.

A person who says that full recovery and full healing and an "undiagnosis" is not possible, they have not seen my journey and they can't speak to who I was years ago versus who I am now. I know I'm a different person...a person who used to have a lot of triggers and now has nearly none. When you're healing trauma, there's definitely grief stages in the midst of that as well. I have a full heart of compassion for those who wish to stay away to protect themselves. Only you can tell where you are in that journey of self-reliance. Just be sure to check in and make sure you're not nurturing something that is already healed. As a heads-up, also beware that those who consider themselves to be "trauma-informed" may not be very Present... Some folks appear like they are supportive, but all they're doing is checking off the box of a trending awareness, using a buzzword to gain business and give off appearances of maturity. Being a Healing Presence to someone's trauma is sacred and immature people tossing buzzwords around can re-traumatize survivors into prolonged digressed healing phases.

   I once had a freak accident at work when a sharp, brand-new xacto knife blade spontaneously went into my finger and sliced it open to the point of needing stitches. Luckily someone caught me with a chair as they rushed to roll it under me before I passed out as I saw the blood drip from my finger. But that was a new experience for me. In all my over 30 years of life at that point, I had never had stitches. I got rushed to a walk-in clinic, got the stitches I needed and then they put one of those splint things on my pinky finger. My boyfriend at the time was so kind. He washed my hair for me because I couldn't get that finger wet and I was also still hyped up on adrenaline and a painkiller. During the healing weeks, I got used to wearing that splint on my finger and I had to do things differently. When it came time to get my stitches out, I found that the first thing I did after that was taken care of and the doctor was turning me loose was, I put the splint back on my finger. And then he looked at me weird but also I noticed it too and I was like *"Oh my God, why did I just do that? I'm just used to it."* This is the perfect illustration of the things we get comfortable with, right? Just because you get comfortable with it or awkwardly comfortable, it doesn't mean that it's right or true or correct or needed. Have we already healed? And we keep thinking we need the splint brace back on our finger that is perfectly whole and fine?

The Call

HEALING JOURNEY CHECKPOINT TECHNIQUE:

Take a moment to get into a quiet, clear space within. Since the subconscious mind works best in pictures, as imagery is the language of the mind, I like to ask my subconscious in meditation to show me a picture that describes where I am on a certain topic. It's surprising what shows up. I said, **"Show me where I am in my healing journey."** In my mind's eye, with my eyes shut, I saw a video clip of an adult riding a little kid's bicycle with the training wheels still on. The knees were painfully knocking on the handlebars even though the adult could get off the bike at any time and carry it with two fingers. This animated visual was the comical confirmation I needed that I was reinjuring myself, thinking that I was still not healed, that I had more healing to do, and by continuing to view myself in an old, expired way, I was living in a self-fulfilling prophecy. The subconscious is saying: **"You've already healed, you've already done the work, and now it's time to see yourself. Stop telling stories that cause you so much pain. You're just bruising yourself over and over again when you can be so much more than what you're allowing yourself to be."**

Have you checked in recently? After all that you've been through, have you checked in to see if you are where you think you are? I'm saying that to help us remember that, Yes, wounds are very real. Yes, re-traumatization hurts deeply. But also- **Is this a memory of the pain or are we actually feeling that pain retriggered again? And can we expand beyond that? After expanding beyond that, can we see how far we've come and maybe we don't have the wounds that we had before?** Eventually, things heal. If you can be around the abrasive person that used to trigger the heck out of you before and you have no charge, you're good. We don't always need to put ourselves back in the same exact place we were before to check and see if our triggers have been healed. A lot of times the universe will bring someone to right where we are and you'll think of that original person who triggered you because this personality is kind of their doppelganger. Not that they look identical, but when they come around, they have the same energy or ways of being, mannerisms or behavior, and you think of that initial occurrence when they're around. It's ok to come apart for a while...but have you noticed how together you are now?

5
YEARNING FOR MORE

Some of us took ourselves off the healing market or the lightworker market because we needed to support ourselves and that is valid. Whether you needed to support yourself financially or emotionally, or some other event descended upon your life that spun you in a different direction, it's humbling. I had to do it myself. It absolutely sucked. At the time, I could not fathom how I was going to balance living expenses and growing a business on the side because I had never paid for myself on my own before. I had been breaking even for over a decade paying for student loans while living with family and the thought of adding more bills on top of that would spin me into a panic attack. A panic attack would also happen at the thought of living with a roommate and all the unknown variables that would bring. I knew I would have one less opportunity to have a panic attack if I just lived alone and dealt with the newness that I had to deal with by supporting myself. My mind had to expand to accommodate double the amount of bills coming out of my account each month, adding grocery shopping, which I had not done before and what that entailed. I wish I had a greater capacity or noticed a greater capacity within me, dug in deep and made myself keep a side business open so that I could be somewhere different now. But that was not what felt natural to me at the time. I packed up my dreams and focused on core, root chakra-level support- physically and financially supporting myself paying living expenses.

Over the years before that, I worked diligently through belief systems to expand to accommodate higher wages. I always wondered and kept asking, the universe for years, *"What is it about me? What's wrong with me? Why do I resonate with such low salaries? Why can't I believe that it's natural for me to have a higher wage?"* Through self-discovery and reprogramming my subconscious mind, eventually the repressed memory started to surface over the course of a year before it was fully remembered, whether I wanted to remember it or not. This repressed memory from childhood was the misalignment that set me on the trajectory of not supporting myself for decades and not believing that I could. In addition to that incident, on several occasions growing up, nearly all my family members said to me at different times, *"I don't know how you're going to support yourself, Leah. You just need to find a man and let him support you."* Meanwhile, internally I was feeling, *"I wanna be an entrepreneur, I wanna have my own business."* but not having the emotional capacity to achieve such means since I had things that I did not remember, that I needed to reframe and heal first. Though these disbelieving statements were made to me over 25 years ago, I was highly impressionable then, way too open to other people's opinions, and struggled to feel my own sense of self in the midst of being aware of everyone else's energies. People's opinions really carried weight for me over my own and it nailed me into a coffin where I could not help myself. Having "thick skin" was a non-reality for me. In fact, sometimes if someone looked at me wrong, I could cry on the spot. Although that's certainly not the case today, it took many years of moulding myself and evolving in order to start having a different experience than that.

There's still people I haven't seen in years who think I'm the same old way. What's frustrating about them is the way they perceive me is incorrect. They read trauma symptoms I had at the time as if I'm an autistic person. They didn't really believe in me being able to achieve my goals and dreams either. There was just a hint of condescension, placating me, playing the role of being an active listener rather than actually seeing my true self underneath layers that had not been healed yet (while psychically, I was aware of their snickers behind my back, thinking I was "special"). Some of you know what I'm talking about. And nobody has really made this point before, but some people who are misdiagnosed as autistic are actually traumatized. They have early childhood trauma, so they develop differently and once you reframe the trauma, the real self can come through. Your voice will change. Your power will align within. And people who have known you your whole life might try to project old versions of you onto you and that's severely frustrating in itself because it's easier to move away and start over having people you don't know see the real new you...who is actually you and been dying to be seen your entire life...but you didn't know why you were showing up the wrong way before.

Anytime I have told the story of repressed memories popping up suddenly then derailing your progress or at least shifting your trajectory to be on that ride for a while, some people get that wide-eyed look in their face like, *"Oh no. Am I missing something?"* Allow me to reassure you that you probably have nothing to worry about, to be honest. Besides, the subconscious mind is so brilliant, it will do what is best for you to ensure your survival, but definitely thrival as much as possible. I look back and see many lucrative opportunities presented itself and the choice is always yours. In the moment, you can choose either to align with the lucrative opportunity even if you're scared and your nervous system freaks out since it's different, or you can choose the opportunity that feels more natural, which is staying the same. There was a period during my healing journey of having a low ambition. I worked part-time while building myself up mentally inside to be the person I wanted to be and not the programmed person coming out of my family's environment. One day, my subconscious was like, *"Hey, remember that thing that happened...It's time to look at that."* and it started peeking through about a year before it fully revealed...right before it was time for me to move out of my parents' house because they were retiring slightly earlier than perceived. There it was, right on cue, as if Divinely planned.

American culture has shifted quite a bit in the last five to eight years due to global events. This is not the same climate it was when I was still living with my family. In some cultures, it's natural for multiple generations of family to be living together and it actually saves everyone money...they can meet their goals faster. But in American culture, there seemed to be a level of hiding it and shame, hoping no one found out while I am psychic and I do hear when people say, *"Oh, that's pathetic. She didn't move out until she was like in her 30s."* Well, I did live with a boyfriend in my 20s but he turned out to be abusive so I came back to my parents' house because that's what I knew and I didn't have any other options due to paying for student loans. So, Yes, it's humbling, but this was my path. It unfolded naturally like this. I didn't have any desire to live with my family for so long, even though I look back at it now as priceless adult bonding time. At 18, I wanted to own my own home and even get a duplex to rent the other side out so that all my living expenses were paid in full...this is way before I ever heard of "Rich Dad, Poor Dad" and that real estate movement. I just always thought with a mindset of *"Work smarter, not harder."* The problem was, I didn't feel like I could, nor that I was *allowed* to do it. It's humbling to put all this out there for you but you have to have the context for where I've been to know what I've been able to achieve. Besides, it's incredibly liberating when you read someone's story and can relate, and I sense there's people reading this, relating to me right now.

My intent is not to talk about my transformation as if past versions of me are who I am today. You'll be no different than past people projecting old versions of me onto me if you're stuck in the wrong space of the story. My point is to shed awareness through my energetic experiences in order to help people gain clarity on the challenges I've had so they can be more aware of the present moment, perceive what's actually going on in weird situations, thus suspend judgment and assuming for intuiting and expanding consciousness. I'm not the only one having energetic experiences they cannot explain...Don't you love a good epiphany?

The yearning for more is always there. There's nothing wrong with that. That's what drives us to grow. That's what drives us to change, even to understand other people if you're wondering why they're showing up differently or why their challenges are seemingly unsurmountable when those seem to not be challenges at all for others. It is through our differences that we appreciate our own journey, seeing it with new eyes and even imagine ourselves in the shoes of another...how far they've come, given what they had to start with that truly pulls community together and enriches our lives. It's uplifting to read a story about someone online or a meme that's heartwarming. But it's way more than that if you physically know them in your community and you've hugged them. You've practiced active listening with them. You care about them. And they pop in your head later personally because you hope they're doing OK with their challenge today. These are personal touches you can't get from being solely an online community. Not that I'm against it, because I reap the benefits of both, but I'm hoping this stirs up your yearning for showing up in person more.

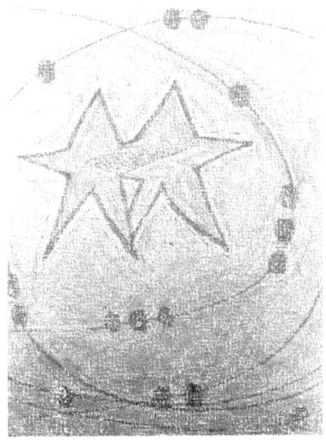

6
PLAYING THE GAME

Growing up, I used to resist labels and stereotypes. I mean, it was the 90s...we were heavily influenced by music that was raging against the machine, literally. It was the next Gen. byproduct of the hippie free love movement decades prior. In 9th grade, I challenged limitations by changing my look on a consistent basis. Some people thought, *"Oh, she's trying to find herself"*, but I wasn't trying to find myself. I was identifying with every version of that self. One day, I would go to school dressed goth. The next day I dressed preppy. The day after that I dressed up in church clothes. Then like a hippie with flare jeans and embroidery down the sides of my pants. A few classmates looked down their nose at me asking why I was doing that and I was like- *"...because I want to"*. A part of them coveted the freedom I felt expressing myself, however I chose and feeling confident in each way. In all actuality of it, I had friends in every single one of those groups of stereotypes...it wasn't really that cliqued out and segregated though. Dressing differently every day also helped spur my creativity. I felt like a new person every day. Sometimes I would part my hair on the left, right, middle or zigzag, or put hair bows in it. And changing my look on a daily basis also inspired other girls to try different things too, so no one was really rigid with their look. I think my unpredictability leveraged me in a way that attracted all kinds of people and interest, but I wasn't trying to get attention. I was experimenting and enjoying my body, trying new things.

By the time I was a senior in high school, colleges were just starting to run aggressive ad campaigns on TV, advertising going to college and it was starting to become the new norm. There really weren't any pharmaceutical commercials at that time, from my recollection. I guess we can check Marion Stokes' archives...she recorded live TV from 1977 until her death in 2012. She started the taping project because she was convinced there was a lot of detail in the news at risk of disappearing forever and by her death, the collection amassed about 71,000 VHS tapes. But I do remember a time before we were bombarded with commercials implying that there's something wrong with us on autopilot and that we need some weird drug we can't pronounce for a disease we didn't hear of until recently because someone made it up or because it's actually symptoms of something else. These commercials are addressing symptoms. They're not addressing the cause. Same with the education ones. They always implied that we were inadequate without their system and their diploma and made grandeur promises of receiving jobs with higher pay at the end of it. The support between college graduation and getting hired didn't really show up in the job market until the last few years. In recent years, we've started seeing where some employers are promising helping graduates pay for their college student loans if they take a job with them. Where was that the last 20 years for me?

Instead, I went to college and I didn't really know what I was signing up for...I didn't see myself as an adult but at the age of 18 you're responsible for signing legal paperwork and I roped myself into 20 years of paying student loans. Gen X and Xennials (Elder Millennials 1977-1983) were heavily impacted by this scheme of promises that were undeliverable. There are some positions that absolutely require college, but if you have a God-given talent, you may not need college. It's nice to have the experience of classes for the structure and accountability. But today's market is completely different, with everyone learning online and free things being on social media.

In American culture, there seems to be this insidious perception that that you're "doing it wrong" if things didn't come out linearly for you. If things didn't go the way you planned, like a master list being checked off 1 by 1 in order: College, Internship, High-paying job, Loans paid off, Marriage, children, etc. I wanted it to...but you know, life is organic, right? And things happen outside of our control. That's one thing I wish I could relay when I applied to jobs because a lot of times there's no room for putting in your own fill-in-the-blank answer. And it's like, *"Well, yes, I'm qualified or I would have your required piece of paper, but I've had these extra challenges that everyone doesn't have."* Some people have had better luck...everything has always worked out for them in a linear fashion and that's great for them. But is anyone reviewing applications and resumes while using their intuition or are they all just looking for the right credentials and linear career experience to be on the resume, painting the picture of your perfect New Hire? I know plenty of people who have the right credentials but do not think logically or with "common sense"...I may not have their credentials, but they're getting hired over me because people are just looking for the right piece of paper to be on the application...the right appearance. Business would flow a lot better if people would use their intuitions because they're missing out on a lot of talent, wisdom and rich life experience through folks who may not have the credentials but have highly efficient minds and adept hearts. Wisdom generates prosperous opportunities and it saves business money. Credentials can often be memorized facts for a piece of paper. But if you're like me, you see through it all. You see the game. Do you want to play the game and pay for a title so you're visible by a corporate job? Or do you want to apply your skillsets to build your own empire?

    We all have different dreams and paths to achieve them...if it is aligned for you to go to college and get those credentials, then you should do it. If there is another way revealing where you wouldn't need to allocate your funds into more schooling, then that way will reveal too. It's not about the money either...Would this experience add value to my life, expand my consciousness? What it boils down to is... Is this my ego making the choice or is this the Divine? Which is making the decision? Remember that when you're playing the game, be sure you're not the one being played.

7
An Early Call

    For some of us, the call came early. I remember having paranormal experiences since I was a kid. I would go to sleep then wake up and realize I was hovering above my body. And then I thought, *"Wow, did that really happen? Well, if it really happened, I'm going to move something so that I know that it happened and I didn't just dream it."* Here I am between the ages of five and seven having this conversation in my head. Let's put it into context. This was like 1989 to 1991. Nothing is on TV about this. Internet is not in every household. Google did not exist. All you had was God within. And if you're lucky, you had an expanded set of encyclopedia in your home, but most people had just a dictionary. So, all I had was inside me to ask questions to discover life. The next time I went to bed, I did what I said I was going to do. I went to sleep, then woke up when I was hovering over my body and moved an object on my dresser and then when I woke up the next morning, I realized it was moved and that I really did move it while I was out of my body. Once I realized that I could do that, the next awareness came- *"Don't tell mom and dad...they don't believe."* I knew their state of consciousness was more limited at the time. No offense to them...there are levels of consciousness. And it would not help me to let them know about it. I also had had a recent experience of a past life memory surface in a dream when I was like 4 or five. I was so excited that I dreamed of me and my dad but I knew it wasn't a dream. I knew it was a former lifetime we had together when we were Native American. I woke up excited to tell him about it, but then he gaslighted me on it and said it was just a dream. Right then I knew he was not awake.

    At that early age, I realized there were different ways of thinking and my family's system was not my system. I was flowing naturally, God was showing me things. I was having paranormal experiences, having angels visit me, sit on the foot of my bed as comfort. And they were blindly talking about believing something that is a system they needed to achieve something with.

While we were in church. I remember asking questions about my parents' belief system. And then it got to the point where they said, *"You're asking too many questions."* Then I would turn to someone else and ask them questions and they would say the same thing. I realized that when somebody said you're asking too many questions, it really meant what they believed was untrue and they had given up on knowing. I tested this with other people using topics besides religion and if they didn't know the answer, they would either lie and make something up that I would be blind sighted by later as false or they would say I'm asking too many questions. Being told you're asking too many questions is not a valid and correct response. That is a byproduct of a lack of maturity, a lack of ownership and sovereignty over one's own mind or simply fatigue. It's a sign of having given up on pursuing true reality and an open door to possible brainwash or default to what's nearby. Remember, it's OK to say, *"I don't know."*

Everywhere you're not willing to be conscious and aware, you're giving up your power. We need to be brave enough to look at those spaces, even if we forgot about them and did them a long time ago. Whenever they reveal, we need to be brave enough to unpack the things that we believe and set it straight. Otherwise, we're putting a Band-Aid on a broken bone. I found that my way of thinking is adored among those who prioritize truth, integrity, right action and my line of thinking is detested and rejected by those who have misaligned priorities and other conflicting energies. I don't see myself as this fairy godmother running around waving her wand to try to clean up everything. But things do tend to reveal that are misaligned, and then I have to perceive whether asking a question will chop off the branch that I'm sitting on, or if it is more aligned to lay low. More gray areas...Yay. I don't have the answers for everything. I do have some solutions. But it requires everyone to start working...start where they are and work what they got. It's a commitment to follow through and then the commitment to circle back if something derails you and then follow through again. Really, we all had an early call...the first call was choosing to come into this human experience to begin with.

8

Breaking the Frequency

We're all in different spaces about truth and integrity. We're all in different places in our lives financially, emotionally, mentally, spiritually. So, when we start working a practice, it is a practice and it doesn't get cleaned up overnight. The efforts we make in the way that we do is good enough because we're all evolving at our at our own appropriate places spaces, and paces. Judgement cuts off awareness. Consciousness includes everything and knows that everyone is where they are and doing the best they can according to their ability to commit and the level of commitment that they've made. We can't go on forevermore saying that all politicians are evil if good people are trying to get in there to start changing that. Then it invokes more negative or dark energy to be combative against the good people that are actually in there trying to change things for the better. We need to be aware that our thoughts are creating. Negative thoughts are like daggers. And positive thoughts are like benevolent angels helping, assisting, protecting, guiding. But more importantly, thoughts, spoken or not spoken, are like a boomerang...they return back to you as well. They might affect people negatively or positively in some way or degree, but they definitely return to you, so choose wisely.

Whether you started answering God's call at a young age or you started answering it at a later age, or it's been intermittent...what matters is that you make it count this time. After all, how much time do we have on this planet? Even after having these core realizations at such a young age, I still gave it a whirl. I gave my parents' belief system the best shot. Instead of partying in college, I was doing something church-related every single night of the week, whether visiting people or volunteer work or meetings or study groups. I squeezed out every last drop of doctrine that I could. I even found a hip-hop church to go to and they had their own flavor on it which was neat. Yeah, it's unique to go to sermon that feels like a hip hop show with turntables spinning and break dancing going on every Sunday. But it was also a belief system that did not explain my visits from angels, my traveling out of body and I was still very intrigued about what that was. Then there's the point I always thought stood out that Jesus made- *"This and greater things you will do"*. I remember having that realization while looking around at the hundreds of people at this mega church and thinking- *"Oh my God...I am the only one here that gets it. I'm reading it right here. This and greater things, you'll do greater things than the miracles that Jesus did."* So, I held that as a founding block of my life quest: **"What else is possible in this reality, on this planet?"** This is long before hearing anything about today's most advanced science which is basically proving God, proving omnipresence. To me, science's "multiple realities" concept sounds like the ability to create miracles. You're shifting in and out of other dimensions and outcomes. What can we do with that to help ourselves and each other? How can we better our lives here? With all this information, are we applying it to better our lives here to end suffering? Have we carved out the time to sit with what we know and ask what are we to do with this? Or are we on autopilot with our loved ones, binge watching TV, working our jobs, doing fun things. And yes, there's nothing wrong with all of that. But if we would like a different experience to show up, we have to carve out time for it. Carve out time for meditation, contemplation, solitude, and sometimes fasting.

Are you ready to answer your intuition? What is that call for you? For some people, the call might be simply getting into therapy because what's been going on hasn't been working for a long time. I like to think about my state of being and ask- *"How long have I felt this way?"* If it's longer than a year, I need do something about it. When I first started asking that question, I realized I had spent most of my life feeling dread when I wake up so I get what it's like to have a chronic condition. Though it may not go away overnight, there are some methods that can give you a boost, speeding up change with ease. For others, you might feel a call to sobriety, change careers, move, pursue a lifelong dream of having a family. Although we may not know what our next thing is, it's important to consider and to sit with as if this quest to find the call is a visitor, a guest in your home. There is a purpose for everyone, and when everyone is living their purpose, will there be a problem left on the planet? Some of us can't even go there, can't even daydream what it would be like to not have a problem to solve.

I would say, let's think about maybe how long you've had a chronic issue, like running out of money or breaking even, feeling lack, struggle, despair, and think about how long you've lived from that pain body space...how that's been your reality for X amount of time. If the problem exists, the solutions exists...they are two sides of a coin. Can you see how there's an infinite array of feelings that can be felt, even opposite of pain...joyful feelings, exuberance, elation, opulence, wealth that also exists simultaneously? All of those feelings are just as readily available for us to feel at any time, if we choose. I'm not mocking you, I'm not saying it's easy if you've been in a painful habit for a long time and nothing has resolved or not much has changed. As the saying goes- *"fake it until you make it,"* and to a degree, the part of that that's true is your subconscious mind does not know the difference between reality and imagined.

VISUAL MANIFESTATION TECHNIQUE:

Close your eyes and imagine a luxury car. Open the car door and lower yourself onto the seat as your nostrils breathe in the aroma of the leather interior. Touch the steering wheel as your gaze meets the rearview mirror, seeing the sun glare from behind you. Notice a stick of gum in the dashboard cubby...unwrap it, smelling its minty fresh flavor on your breath as you insert it into your mouth and tastebuds salivate on your tongue.

If you were to rehearse this over and over and over, eventually at some point you would find yourself in that scenario physically. This is how people manifest. You have to make it real for you. Now, whether you own that car or are simply invited to sit down and try it on, that's another story. Maybe there's other visuals you add to it, like seeing the title in hand with your name on it, or a slip with the words PAID IN FULL.

With that in mind, as painful as it is to have the same experience over and over and feel like nothing ever changes and nothing will ever change, we have to change that narrative and imagery inside for it to change out there. If it's financial limitation, we have to break the frequency of feeling what we feel when we log into our bank account expecting it to be the same limited total but in meditation, start visualizing a doubled total and adding to it. We have to stop the feeling of dread when we wake up in the morning by noticing other spaces and having the awareness that you can feel something different upon waking. Even if it started with that same dread feeling, you can change it in the moment and create a new habit of positive anticipation and gratitude each morning upon waking.

We have to break the frequency of the same for something new to show up. Some of us have not broken the frequency of abusive relationships, of being disrespected at our jobs, of hating politics.

Whatever that thing is to you, decide what you're going to break the frequency of. The problems are inside before they are outside. It may seem like they showed up outside, but it is how we feel about them that determines whether they are a problem or not. If we feel limited, we will experience limitation. If we feel liberated, we will experience liberation. We are directing our lives by what we feel inside, and although some people may be in a lower space and think that I'm blaming them, I invite them to put down the daggers and take some breaths.

BREAKING THE FREQUENCY TECHNIQUE:

Scan your body and see where you feel injustice, that urge to blame me (or the messenger) for the things that have happened to you or for your life's current state. Breathe into that catch or that lump in your throat and invite your favorite Healer in...maybe it's Jesus Christ. Invite the Healer to begin shifting that chronic energy entanglement that has been there the same way over and over and ask for a healing: **"I ask for this healing in the name of Jesus Christ. I asked for the Christ healing energy to infuse this block that seems like it will not change, that my thoughts won't change, that my feelings won't change, that I'm stuck in an autopilot same draining experience and please override me and all of this with grace and ease to experience something different and better, please. Thank you, God."** It might be helpful to visualize a healing energy like a ball of light that looks like the sun as it comes in. It could be the color that you first picture in your mind. Infuse that affected area in your body or mind with that color. Expand it out. What does it feel like? Does it feel like love? Does it feel like peace? Does it feel like joy? Does it have a feeling? Do you sense a cool or a heat sensation along with it or not? Is it more like a vacuum just sucking up all the bad? **"All the cause, effect, record, memory, thoughts and feelings of things that have not changed for so long that you desperately desire and need to change for the better, let that vacuum suck it all out with grace and ease out of your mind. We're talking mental constructs. We're talking expectations and feelings. We're talking worst-case scenario creation...especially the kind that happened on autopilot."**

Allow the vacuum experience to continue. Catherine Ponder calls it The Vacuum Law of Prosperity. She was talking about getting rid of things physically in your home that no longer serve a purpose but I like to apply that concept internally, mentally, emotionally and energetically. We have to get rid of the way we think in order to have a different experience, breaking that vicious cycle of thinking and feeling if the way we think has been about breaking even, always running out of money, or expecting to be disrespected by others. Someone who has an opulent amount of money coming in, double the amount needed, required and desired would not be thinking those thoughts. Same goes for being respected.

For some of us, The Call is to first, realize the possibility of something new coming in... that it is possible to experience a different reality besides pain. As we're letting this energetic exchange take place, this healing, this miraculous anointing within The Call, vacuuming up the things that prevent us from feeling the possibilities, Let's circle back to the thought that your subconscious mind will believe whatever you tell it...whatever you feel and visualize to be real. If you would like to feel like you just won the lottery, maybe it's the lottery version of something, right? You have a breakthrough or you get a windfall of success, maybe someone you've dreamed of being with shows up...it could be a love relationship, or a friendship, but their energy is so healing for you and such a contribution to you...not in a vampire way, like you're sucking everything out of them, but it's mutually beneficial to each other in ways you never dreamed possible. **No matter how many years you have spent** wishing for this breakthrough but not getting it and desire somebody to contribute to you in a positive way...even if you're coming out of a period of users and abusers mooching off of you and tapping you for their benefit, and you're been getting sucked dry....

Allow yourself this space right now that's freshly vacuumed from all anti-dreams. This is your seed space inside. This is your manifestation portal here we're talking about. You might sense the space in your mind's eye area or in your heart or you can hold your hands facing each other, as if you're holding an energy ball if it helps you. Be present with this space, wherever that is for you. I have used all three at different times, it just depends on how it is showing up for me.

So here we have whoever our healer is, like Jesus Christ, Saint Germain, Archangel Michael, Mary Magdalene...our team, who is our dream team of Angels, Ascended Masters, Ancestors, perhaps a native medicine man. Allow your dream team to reveal- They're here to help you. They could be from your soul lineage, from different lifetimes. They're here to help you transcend and raise your own consciousness, raise your own frequency. That's what we're doing here. Cause the drama of the past is done at last. We can't keep moving forward with limited thoughts and feelings- that experience is done. You've learned everything on this level, you've squeezed the lemon dry. There's nothing left to squeeze out of the painful experiences you've been in, so it's time to be done with it. You have to choose. You had to put your foot down and say I'm done with it. *"As long as it's aligned with Divine Order, show me how I'm done with it."* And then feel elated like you were as a child. Everything was provided for you. You didn't have to worry about anything. You're playing all day, the food showed up, you ate, you got presents at your birthday and Christmas...everything was always provided for-someone would take you shopping for clothes. And if you didn't have these experiences in childhood due to hardship or other ways of growing up, allow yourself to have these feelings now...implant these memories into your subconscious. What would it feel like if you had that? Spend as much time as you need on each one. You could spend an hour on this visualization and if you've had missing experiences, lacking rather than benevolent.

I recommend spending more time inserting these seeds into your subconscious so that you do feel safe because it's usually the inner child- the parts of us that were missing information and missing support in the past-that derail our adult experiences in the present. The inner child literally acts out but it's showing up as you as an adult, so you look like the jerk. We have to get ahead of our inner child's rebellion... wherever they weren't seen or heard, wherever they weren't believed or they were punished when it wasn't their fault. All of that, we just allow the Vacuum Law of Prosperity to come and remove those wounds because we can't move forward with them. They have to move on. It's time to ascend. It's time to be wealthy. It's time to be healthy. It's time to live our lives as a sovereign being having a human experience. To be sovereign, you have to see that you are sovereign, that you have choice. Free Will is yours. And once you see it, then you can remember you have choice and what would you like to choose.

Being present to the sensations in your body, we're still working with this...right now my hands are shoulders apart because my energy ball got really big as I'm writing this and my hand is moving like a fishtail. The energy is moving and changing in me and in you, and we're evolving. This is a great healing. If you weren't awakened to a call before, you might find yourself receiving now. Thank you, please. And if it's not Divine Order for anything to shift for you, it won't. God is in control here.

One of the biggest mistakes that metaphysical people can make is to think that because God is a part of them, within them, that is it is all up to them and that co-creation is not needed anymore. But I will remind you that it is a collaboration like Yin and Yang, of Free Will and Divine Will. Sometimes it's out of our control. And sometimes our ego thinks it is all our control, that it's all up to us. There have been many times before I was awakened to the metaphysical, where I had no idea how things would work out and I felt like I was a loser, but I won instead. I thought I was unworthy, but I got something even better than I thought I could. It was a windfall success. There was no part in that timeframe where I was micromanaging my feelings in order to manifest the right outcome. God will go above and beyond to override your unworthiness, to make sure you get what's yours, in the perfect timing. Know that even though we're becoming more aware of our God power, fine tuning our feelings to manifest through the law of attraction consciously, it is not all up to us. Thank God. It is not all on us, Thank God. By all means, I'm not saying if you lose your job to stop job hunting and just give it all up to God- that's not what I'm saying at all. But if you've done everything that you know to do and you do not expect to be laid off and suddenly you are, when you panic, panic. Feel what you feel. Let the emotions purge out of you, let the panic come out, let the fear come out and then find your way back into gratitude. It's like, *"Thank you God for this working out, even though I don't know how it's going to work out. Thank you God for your Divine Order Call. Thank you, God, for your will being done. Thank you, God, for your support, for your real, actual, tangible financial support. Thank you for expected and unexpected income before I need it. And thank you for plenty to eat and plenty to share. And thank you for all my bills paid in full. And thank you for bills being paid ahead."* **There is grace- receiving good things we don't deserve, there is mercy- not receiving bad things we do deserve, and there are blessings- an abundance of both.**

Years ago, Japanese Artist, Wakuneco, wanted a purpose…an idea that was unique and different for her to create for a living. She prayed for a purpose then the idea came to create these stunning needle-felt cat portraits. Using just wool, identical to the cat's fur and a needle, Wakuneco crafts unbelievably realistic 3D pet portraits by commissions around the world. She was featured on a Netflix documentary called "Cat People" for this uniqueness. **Just when you think "everything has been done under the sun", a new creative method is born. Never give up, never assume. Reach deeper within to birth something new.**

9

RECOGNIZING THE CALL

Part of recognizing the call is knowing that you're part of it. You're not all of it. You're showing up, you're hearing it, you're seeing it, you're taking action on what's yours to do in that moment. And then you let go of what's not yours. It is an ebb and flow and it's scary sometimes. It's also been said that the subconscious mind doesn't know the difference between fear and excitement. What if when we had fear, we feel that. Be genuine about it...it's not stuffing it under a rug. But also see how much it has in common with excitement and start celebrating. Jump up and down. Act as if it's already resolved. Get on the other side of it, act as if it's already here. Turn on that song, "Break on through (to the other side)" by The Doors and dance your heart out while visualizing in detail: accounts paid in full, balances increasing by 10s of thousands, having more money in your account than you've ever experienced before, being loved fully by someone who is a being of love no matter how many abusive people you've fallen for before...and even visualizing deeper down on the energetic level, Archangel Michael cutting ties with his giant healing sword between you and all karmic relationships, energies, associations, limitations- They do not serve you...the ones that kept pulling you back in for Round 5 in the Ring of Heart-Lashing, musing, *"...maybe they're the one cuz they keep coming back."* Your life is yours to create...you don't need another round of abuse to prove you exist. Just because you feel connected to someone, it doesn't mean it's Divine for you to pursue. Sometimes you have to cut energetic ties with them...and multiple times. I don't mean physically. Sometimes even in my own family, we've had misaligned connections to the point where there was overreach in each other's lives. Overreach isn't freedom. That's being dominated by each other. No one likes being dominated by another person to the point of not having any Free Will or feeling like you can only create but a very small fraction of what you want to create because that person's energy flow is sitting on top of you. I have seen this pattern a lot in couples where the woman is a strong, dominating force and the male is a meek or humble energy. Although it's not the case in every dynamic, sometimes the woman has used their projections to energetically trap the man into the relationship. It's kind of like how some women have physically trapped a man with pregnancy, only they are energetically trapping the man with their overreaching intentions into the man's world almost like a spider web. This type of man needs to have healthier boundaries to have a strong sense of self. It's great to have an open heart and to be a kind and loving being, but everyone does not have your best interest in mind.

These are weird energetic issues that I've realized on my journey of awakening and I've had to adjust even though we weren't taught these things in school and I feel like a big weirdo for writing a book about it... it needs to be done. I'm answering my Call. People have questions that have not been answered and they don't think they can be answered because they just shrug them off with cognitive dissonance flooding their worlds thinking, *"Oh well, guess it's nothing."* Would you like to stop gaslighting yourself? Would you like to start acknowledging the experiences you're having and have answers for them, overcome them, create greater than them? I do. This is why I haven't given up after decades of wrong relationships because I was watching the energy patterns and realizing how much erroneous control others' energies had over me before. I was too open to others' energies so I had to begin the process of closing up to them, gaining sovereignty over my energy field, setting proper boundaries internally, energetically. And then of course, you get tested by going back into collaboration with them, being around the former overreachers again to see if you get duped by it, infiltrated again then reinforcing more boundaries and setting up those new ways of being. When you show up differently, things out there have to show up differently. When your energy inside has changed, what shows up out there has to change. This is cause and effect. This is the mirror.

Sometimes the change happens by answering The Call, beginning the step of action because the universe wants to see if you've got skin in the game..."*If you can get started on this project, then XY and Z will happen next."* I have often thrown myself into the fire just to see if I would burn. Not a literal fire, but one time I didn't know if I could do psychic readings for people on the spot, even though I read people psychically all the time. I got invited to do this podcast based out of the UK. And I said, *"Alright, sink or swim, let's give it a shot."* So, I did. I showed up and images revealed, thoughts and feelings came. People confirmed them. And it was done. I did several shows. I only stopped because I felt like a hypocrite when my cousin died by suicide. I felt like a fraud...It's not my fault that he died...most of the time people like that have been thinking about ending life for over 5 years. A psychic I once consulted with said that there wasn't really anything I could have done to change his mind, that I need to move on from this. Then he told me the sign that shows up to let me know that everything's fine. I need to move on from this. Time to pick it back up and move forward.

I know some of you are like me too, very sensitive and aware. And I will say, just because you're aware of something, it doesn't mean you're responsible for it. OK? It's not your fault if you're aware of something in your consciousness because you are psychic. You cannot control the outcomes of other people. It is not your job to control the outcomes of other people. It is not your job to save the world. You can show the light and if they choose to save themselves, they will. But there's a rewiring that needs to take place here because religion wants you to think that you have to go out and save others, and that's what's hurting people. People are wired wrong, thinking that they're supposed to fix everything *out there*, change everything *out there*. If more people would stop looking *out there* and start looking *inside first*, then we'll stop putting the cart before the horse. When things are in order, we can live in order and create more order that's harmonized with a universal flow of light, love, and prosperity.

If your internal, energetic "metaphysical vacuum" is still running, dear...**Allow it to dry your tears. Because I know it just did mine. Allow it to usher that garbage bag full of pain from all that you perceived before and could not change and could not help.** It was out of your control yet the urge to control it was there. And you're exhausted. Because it wasn't yours to do anything with, just let it go. With grace and ease, let it all go and call your energy back in. Everything that we're removing from us, we have to replace it with something. So allow your Healers to replace it with more love and light. In your mind or body where you're releasing stuck energy, you can visualize it's a garden having been weeded out...the dirt nourished and stirred...your favorite bushes, plants, flowers, trees planted in place of weeds. And remember, your breath in this space is here. Breathe comfortably. Breathe slowly and deeply as it is comfortable for you. With each relaxed breath in and out...nourish the soil, water the soil, sunlight the soil. **Allow the spaces in your mind and body that were just relieved from such deep heartache and pain to be**

fully filled. Nourished. Comforted. Solaced. Reassured. Commended. Supported. Now with every in breath, we're even deeper connected to God, the Divine. And deeply healed and restored. With that same breath in and out, releasing the old and allowing the new.

To God be the glory for all this change. If that phrase just triggered you because it sounds religious, I invite you to also surrender that trigger. Maybe you have an Anti-Christ Entity that's bothering you. Allow your Healing Guides to escort Anti-Christ Entities out of your manifestation spaces, out of your energy field for reform as Light. It's important to look at what we see as a trigger. I've had this conversation with people who don't like the word God and they would rather switch to The Universe or Source Creator. And while it's important to forge new ways when you free yourself from religious doctrine, I find that the energy is still tangled in something that has a trigger, and eventually you'll need to circle back and reframe that.

Did you know there are religious entities guarding each religion to make sure people stay in line? There is nothing Divine about them...they are not from God. They might as well be demons. But they wish to ensure that you're enslaved by them. This is why some metaphysical people have allowed themselves to be programmed back into organized religion. Some religious entity got in (usually unhealed guilt or trauma) and now they've digressing back into a box instead of owning their God power within. More common than not, a lot of these people have children. It's important for the developmental growth of children to be in a community surrounded by people their age. This is good programming that instills in them the expectation that they always have a community. When they become adults, then they expect that community is natural. The environment a child grows up in becomes the baseline expectation for their adulthood. I've seen more times than not, parents taking their children out of a metaphysical church they feel aligned with simply because there was no children's program available to them there. They would rather indoctrinate their families into a limited religious belief system that had a children's program just so that children have the experience of community rather then forge it alone as the only family with children in a spiritual community. Do you feel the call to start a children's program in *your* metaphysical community?

If your mind and energy are enslaved by a religious belief systems, you won't truly and fully know God and know that God is here in every space that you take up and every breath that you breathe and that miracles are unfolding on a whim and at your will because in order to have religion,

The Call

you have to have a belief system. And if you have a belief system, you have to give your power to the belief system. So if you give your power to the belief system, then you no longer have the power within you to create miracles like Jesus did and greater, as he said. When you think about it, would you like to create miracles? And then the thought comes, *"Well, who am I to create miracles? I'm not God."* Well, that's the belief system that comes with the religion that wants to keep you trapped in that box to never use your Healing power.

But if everybody is a spark of God, then that spark of God is the power of God that we have within...The Free Will and the Sovereignty to use at will aligned with Divine Order, harming none, helping ourselves and each other. Would you like to give up that statement and belief system *"Well, I'm not God."*? What if that's the only one locking the door to infinite possibility and ease with change and prosperity? What if instead of you hunting jobs down, the jobs hunted you down? What if it's the difference between that? Would you like to notice that you are the key to unlocking that experience for yourself? If we know...once we know that we have the power to choose, then the next question is, well, what do I want? What if there's a greater collaboration asking of us, that when we ditch the linear flow, we are organically in tune to intuit it. I'm not saying answering The Call is easy, especially not after the massive amount of change internally, personally and globally we have all experienced in the last few years. That's a lot for a human life, let alone a handful of years. But what I do feel called to highlight is that there is a call for every person. There is a calling, a purpose. And just like one candle lights the other, That's what I'm here to be and do. The rest is up to you.

10

Answering the Call

When you think about answering The Call, what does that feel like? Joy. Anxiety. A mix. When you think about inviting other people to your purpose and sharing your wisdom, what comes to mind? Does a worst-case scenario come up to block you from moving forward?

ENCASING IT WITH CHRIST CONSCIOUSNESS TECHNIQUE

As that surfaces within, scan your body. Do you feel it in your jaw? Is it in your mind? Is it a ping in your heart? Encase that area with Christ Consciousness. Allow this loop of energy to cease to be embedded in your field, to cease being connected to your call unrealized and unactualized. Allow yourself to see its attachment has been removed from you. All the feelings that it's still here are melting away, all the memories that it's associated with are transforming. All the anchor points have been removed. Keep working with this visualization and feelings until all the limited feelings have transformed from your body and mind.

When you picture your internal spaces, you should see a clear image, whatever that looks like to you...whether a blank white room or a bright sunny day shining through a window...something that resembles a confirmation that it is done. That worst-case scenario thought and feeling loop has ended and will not bother you anymore. It does not block your taking action on your call no matter how big or small. Your call might be to support someone else's call...it's not always a solo journey of creation. Some of our dreams collaborate together and overlap a little. Allow your mind and body to expand to receive what this is for you with grace and ease. May you be in a new space about your call if you're coming back to it and you had to move away from it for a while or you got distracted or pushed off your course. Let's come back to center. The call may be different or the same. Everything that was here before, maybe regrets or painful feelings of not being seen or heard, challenges that overrode your authority, or misrepresenting yourself accidentally. We're stepping out of those experiences and stepping into your higher state of vibration with ease. Even if people think that you're a newbie but you're actually an advanced soul...even if others' infiltrated energy flows caused you to look like a minion when you're actually an expert in your awareness of a topic. The past is behind us and we're moving forward from this point, answering The Call. Rising up, doing what is ours. Being more of your soul. Grounding yourself. Growing yourself.

For some people who are still on their call, who have not stopped, maybe they took a metaphysical curve where they became so esoteric they can't have a normal conversation with an average person anymore. I invite those people to answer The Call of integrating more with this human experience. Grounding yourself. If you can't have a surface-level conversation with a regular person without talking like a woo-woo star person, why are we on this planet? Are we trying too hard to be different rather than finding our middle space with a gift? Do we have a specialness syndrome? If we feel like we are too different, are we? If we are steering too hard into being different in order to feel special or to project superiority over others who have not awakened yet, do we have a superiority complex?

Whenever we refuse to be aware of something, we are choosing to have blind spots or limitations. It is where our new glass ceiling begins to develop. People who create such walls around them as if they are too woo-woo to relate to regular people anymore, they have an imbalance and are refusing to grow. As exaggerated and egoic walls of specialness and superiority complexes began to crumble, we'll be able to see more clearly how our purposes collaborate with each other. As walls of self-importance and over-exaggerated differences dissolve into a balanced wholehearted purpose-driven intention, growth can begin to occur. If we're not evolving, we're stuck. That's usually when people start stealing from and competing with others, living from the outside in rather than going within to get renewed. Stealing and competing is taking a shortcuts at other people's expense, as if you are superior to them and they mean nothing. But the more people evolve, the more people become adept in reading others. As their natural psychic abilities develop, you will not be able to hide your malicious intent towards others. You will not be able to hide behind false pretenses and false confidence.

When you answer The Call, it feels exciting. It's like *"Oh wow! I know what I am here to do"* or *"This excites me!"* There's a lot of enthusiasm up front and we may not be looking at what might arise. Family patterns can come up...the energies that try to derail your purpose. It's not all happening through you either...it's not all in your mind. Sometimes it shows up through other people...like lightworkers against you out of jealousy or ministers trying to pump you for content because they've stopped growing inside and they're on the borderline of burn-out so they take shortcuts. It's strange...you would think people who are on the path of being a lightworker or a metaphysical spiritual leader...you would think that they would have a handle on their intentions and why they were doing the things that they are doing, but some people have ingrained patterns and ways of being that are atrocious. The patterns are against the very intention that they held for their mission and their ministry. It absolutely makes them appear to be a hypocrite, undermines their authority, and makes them look like a fraud.

One example of this is we're all daydreaming, talking about the things we love and I'm about to share my point of view when someone intuited what I was about to say and then destroyed it with negativity word for word about how much he hates this and that. And those were the very same sentences I was about to say that I loved and I looked forward to having. Given the dynamic we had of him holding dominance over my energy, I did not feel empowered to stand up to him. Even though it was just a casual conversation and it was kind of flippant the way he said it, I still felt like his words were a cannonball bursting through my chest, keeping me silent. No matter what I did, I could not get away from the feeling that I had no control over my life, no authority over my choices. This went on for decades. I don't think it fully began releasing until after his death, even though I had been working on it and had received many healing sessions over the years to address it and gain my power back. After a few years of healing and rebalancing my energy flows, I finally had an epiphany that I needed to go live in the mountains. This was the very thing that his toxic energy had intuited psychically and destroyed as if I could never achieve it and I wasn't allowed to. If he were here today, he would not remember ever saying anything negative and he would not agree with me on this. He would say, *"Of course you're allowed to do what you want to do. You're an adult."* But that just goes to show how unaware people are of the things they're saying, what they're feeling, energies they're embodying and expressing and why. It does have a gaslighting element to it as well, but they don't see themselves so it's just where they are in their awareness and they certainly don't see their impact on others. **It takes time for people to: 1. Be willing to see, but**

2. Cut through the BS, the cognitive dissonance then 3. Have a massive amount of forgiveness for themselves for saying and doing things that they adamantly said that they had never done and would never do. If you are truly committed to expanding consciousness and ascending your soul, you can't get there from there. You have to let go of the old stuff. You have to let go of the dark stuff and you can't scoot it under the rug like entitled influencers think they can...hiding it with an angle or a filter online. Energy doesn't lie. People see the truth, whether you think they do or not, and whether you're willing to see it about yourself or not.

The challenge with today's young adults is the fact that most have been raised on social media and nobody has been setting ethical parameters. When you can make money being an influencer online, it's up to the individual to set their own moral compass. And what happens if they don't have a moral compass? Then you have people going around influencing other people by projecting a polished image while achieving success in divisive ways. I hate to sound like an old person, but in today's time, it really is challenging for elders to feel respected since everyone can just Google everything or wave an AI wand on it on a whim. It seems like people with life experience are just thrown out the window. There was a time where you would look to your elders to ask them about their life experience with something and those inquiries seem to be going extinct, having been replaced by technology. This is another breakdown of community. While older is not always wiser, there's some things you certainly learn by living and not looking up online.

I wish that social media would not call it "Friends" on your list and call it "Connections" instead. When social media first rolled out, it *was* your friends that you added online. But over time, people started using social media for business. Then it became a business platform to let everyone on board onto your friends list. And you want to be kind, so you let people in. And also you might be curious to make a new friend, so you let them in and they're on your "Friends" List. But what I found disappointing is most people just want to collect followers and they don't want to collect more friends. They make surface level efforts to get to know you or be your friend and that's even done online...they don't even make the effort to meet you in person and spend time with you and be in your Presence. These people are simply wanting your business...they don't want your friendship. And it's subtle, but sometimes people are posting what seems to be vulnerable, personal stories, but instead they are projecting an influencer version of themselves as a wall, giving off a false sense of personal connection when what they're doing is attempting to sell an image or a persona in attempts to increase their business profits. It's really confusing on social media when you had a personal page that family uses as an online photo dump, but now it's being used for business and people have a blurred sense of what friendship really is because even though you're called "Friends" online, they're not being a very good friend (yes, I know you could always get a business page, dump all acquaintances from your personal page but the culture still needs addressing– the problem is the lack of awareness about false connections and behaviors that's breaking down society).

Do we remember what it's like to be a friend? Growing up, I knew my friends because they had been to my house and asked to see my photo albums and art archives. Those are the only people who ever got to see them because they cared to ask. Now, in a culture of sharing and oversharing, we are over-stimulated by so much content and the lines have been blurred for too long that people don't know how to be a real friend anymore. They don't know how to make real connections. They don't know who their real friends are. This is very disconcerting because it takes friends to build community. I mean, you can make friends at a community, but you have to have real connections, real conversations, real present moments in order to call someone a friend. And this is a topic that is a super gray area because I do have friends I've had for a long time that we don't see each other on a daily basis nor talk to each other very often but when we meet up, we do still have a genuine level of care for each other though we live far apart- that's not what I'm talking about in this moment. What I'm talking about in this moment is the sense of entitlement people have for being on your "Friend's List". There's a false sense of deeper connection with you when in actuality, what's happened the last decade or more is social media has made all of us our own paparazzi, while wondering why we don't have deeper relationships with each other. And I feel like everyone is kind of in a fog about it. Nobody's really talking about it- this is also why I'm bringing it up, to take the rug out, beat the dust out of it and sweep out everything that has been jammed under there the last 20 years. No one is really that happy and satisfied with this gray area unless you just genuinely wish to be left alone or enjoy gossip, being "in the know", and are doing control.

I think everyone could benefit from a true friend that you can tell everything to and know that it's not going to get around to a bunch of people you've never met before. In my book, a trustworthy person is someone you don't have to tell them, *"Hey, will you keep this between us"* because they're aware enough to know that what is shared between two people stays between them, and if there is something to be done with that information, your intuition would tell you, or you can clarify with each other on that. Whether the moral decline has occurred as a byproduct of social media or the absence in church attendance, we still need basic morals to keep the world flowing kindly and in a civilized manner. We still need the parameters, rules that keep Divine Order in place, and harmony on the planet. Without them, you have influencers thinking that their entitlement is confidence. And instead of taking a compliment and being kind to others, they act like, *"Yeah, duh. I'm worth it."* This kind of behavior is mean and vindictive. **That's not confidence... it's entitlement. Entitlement is not of the light. Entitlement is not worthiness. It is vain. It is worthiness overshadowed with ego. We need to take the ego out and put God back in.**

Some people think that answering The Call means it is the beginning of a cakewalk and then they get to live their life happily ever after, like a fairy tale. Just like grief and healing, is not linear...it is cyclical. **You don't answer The Call and everything is perfect sunshine and rainbows the rest of your life. You answer The Call and then you purge the darkness. Answer The Call, purge the darkness. Answer The Call, purge the darkness. Answer The Call, purge the darkness.** It is a continual choosing over and over and shifting trajectory from where we thought we were to where we actually are and where we actually are to where we aim to be and it's revealing in live feedback as we continuously correct what we are seeing show up for us and align with what we would rather be headed towards. It is a process of reform...a stitching and weaving, in and out, ebb and flow tapestry of our life. There is no perfection but the messy imperfection process that we are as we are. This is why the dream comes to us as we are. We are ready recipients to receive it. It would not be delivered to you falsely or untimely before you were ready. It was delivered to you when you were ready and it is reiterated to you. Now is the time. Shake off your fear of being judged. Shake off the old versions of you in your mind. Shake off what community issue you had before. It's time to walk through that door and answer The Call. You're not here to breathe and die and do nothing in between. Step up and take your place...take up your space. Expand your being beyond your challenges, beyond the past and be who you came here be... and in order to do so, humility is needed...Grace, Peace, Kindness...Human*kind*.

11
PUTTING THE KIND IN HUMANKIND

We need to put the kind back in human*kind*. Even if you don't believe in a God, you can at least overlap with *that*...that *kindness* makes the world go round. It is true that if you need a breakthrough, *give* a breakthrough. One time I needed to get hired and I didn't know what to do since time was running out for the deadline of moving out of that home and I needed more income to support myself. After having applied to many jobs and sitting there waiting to hear back for an interview, I thought about my circles-Who do I know? Does anybody need help? It's often random acts of kindness (while detached to outcome) that sends ripple effects, positive energies back to you when you need it. And who knows, it might come back in the form of a job interview. It suddenly occurred to me that my family member did not have a means of transportation. Their only means of transportation, which was their bicycle, was wrecked when they were hit by a car. I knew what I could do...I bought them a bike and had it mailed to their house. They had to put it together, but it was a breakthrough. Could they have bought their own bike? Maybe. But you know, when we go through hardship, sometimes there's a part of us that wants us to suffer. Like, *"Yeah, I deserve that."* even though you don't deserve that. You have to see your own worthiness and let yourself learn from mistakes and let yourself feel like you've paid enough, feel like you deserve to move on from bad experiences in order to support yourself or expand enough to let something better happen. Sometimes you get so ingrained in self-punishment, you need someone else to break the frequency of that routine and flow of energy. You need a breakthrough. So, if you need a breakthrough, you give a breakthrough. When I gave that person a breakthrough, they were elated and their joy was off the charts for the first time in a long time. It was unexpected. It wasn't their birthday, it wasn't for Christmas, it was just because. And there's kind of a sticky

The Call

place where people say don't do something in order to get something. But also it is true that if you *need* a breakthrough, *give* a breakthrough. There is a level of detachment where you can invoke a resolution to come out of a situation by giving to others. It just so happened that it was the medicine for me at the time. Giving this person a breakthrough caused me to manifest the job offer and home that I needed to move out right in the nick of time. It is simply the act of giving that we're impressing upon the formless universe, saying that *"this is correct behavior that we like to receive"* and when you're neutral about it, that act will come back to you in the Divine Order timing that is meant. If you don't think that you're actually clicking with what I'm saying, sit in meditation with this concept and ask God to show you how to perceive this.

Some people have been entitled for so long, they don't know that they are not exhibiting confidence. Entitlement is not a healthy feeling. It's not supportive. It's not inclusive. And it's the beginning of "pride comes before a fall". What I have learned is if you run into a group of people who have a common vibe of entitlement, it's best to walk away from them instead of poking the hornets' nest. Usually entitled people think they know everything, and if they know everything, they're not willing to see. If they're not willing to see, they have massive blinders on. And if they have massive blinders on, then they think they know everything and everything's good. So, it's like a self-fulfilling prophecy that keeps everything the same and if you're the one difference that they're not ready for, they didn't ask for, they didn't want there, then you're setting yourself up for a war of energetics, of spiritual attack and downright unwarranted vindictiveness against you. I've been in a group before where they claimed to be eliminating mean girl culture and yet they were the very ones being the mean girl to me because they felt inferior to me. Yes, my perspective is expansive, but I didn't say I was better than them because I have easier ways of doing things and epiphanies. This is just how I'm wired and I'm giving freely to help people, so why would somebody attack someone who's giving freely to help people? I thought we could do business together, but what this person wanted to do was squish me down under them, dominate me and make me seem like I was their minion. At this point, the only thing left for me to do was to leave their group because they weren't living in integrity, they weren't being kind to me, and their followers thought they were the greatest. One day those people will wake up when they're ready to see, but as long as they continue to hold this person on a pedestal, they won't be able to see it- they're too close to it.

The Call

Some people won't be willing to see that *they are the mean girl* they're trying to eliminate in the culture. They have built their follower count for years, so they desperately don't want to be seen in a bad light, thus never admit the epiphany that they were attacking me. But that's even a prideful thing to do. The ego will make somebody want to cut down their group members so that they remain on the highest point of the pyramid. But if you're not the highest point of view, the most aware point of view, then you're stagnating your group's growth as well as your own. If I had an online group and someone had a more enlightened point of view than me, I would say, *"Wow, Love that! Thank you for sharing!"* I wouldn't hide their memes from the feed...I do not nourish my ego- I keep it in check. It actually empowers people to see your humanness, that you don't have to "keep up appearances" of being the most aware one in the group, even if it is your group. Some people are so egoic they'll read this statement and then act like it was their idea and then their followers who are still blinded will believe them as if it's their idea and that's still ego even though they're reforming a little bit, a little nudge of a trajectory is being made...they're still nourishing their ego because they're not giving credit where it came from.

Don't you get that the human experience is more like a relay race? We should be passing the baton to each other, not engaging in a Spartacus war of throwing medieval torture devices at each other and tossing each other to the lions (energetically). If that's how you see life and you're being cutthroat with other people, you're still purging a lot of 3D lower density energies from your family lines. You'll get there eventually, but if you want to grow faster...and usually, the ego does want to compete and achieve...if you want to grow faster, you'll want to transmute those energies and stop being that way a lot faster with ease. It's not a race, of course...it's actually a very big disservice to not be present to your process. If you have something heavy coming up, you can't speed through it...you have to deal with it and it might come up more than once because some things are embedded. Some things take more than one pass at it to clear completely. That's why this is not an ego experience. It's a "surrendering of the ego" experience on this planet.

Another reason it's good stay open is sometimes it looks like someone is having an ego moment when they're actually exhibiting trauma symptoms, or are under psychic attack, or are experiencing both at the same time that give the appearance of being less aware or incompetent. It sucks not to be seen or heard and have a whole community of people assume that you're an incompetent newbie in spirituality when you're actually an advanced being whose human body and mind are having a certain temporary challenge. But the way to heal injustice is to not focus on injustice, because that creates more experiences like it. The way to heal injustice is to create ways to be seen and heard, create ways to call out the evil and hold others accountable with ease, create ways to set standards where they need to be. And that's the point of my call here.

ENTITLEMENT REFORM TECHNIQUE:
Everywhere you thought God was advising you, but ego was...
Breathe into those spaces with ease.
Scan your body. Allow truth to reveal.
As ego is exposed, surround it with love.
Expand to embrace truth.
Breathe into restriction, dissolving pain and fear into oneness.

Everywhere you feared ego was advising you, but it was God instead...
Breathe into those spaces with ease.
Scan your body. Allow truth to reveal.
As God is revealed, release fear with love.
Expand to embrace truth.
Breathe into restriction, dissolving pain and fear into self-love,
Support.

All delusion dissolves under grace in a miraculous way.
All right action and aligned insight is all that remains.
Go in peace.

12
CLARIFYING INTENTIONS

Yes, I do have high standards. I don't expect everyone to choose them. My mind naturally thinks in terms of seeing a problem, breaking it down into actionable steps as a solution. Some people find themselves feeling inferior or assume I'm projecting inadequacies on them. What I offer is for those who are ready and willing. But I get that once you see something, you can't unsee it. Then you're often left to deal with the aftermath of having been introduced to an easier way, contrasted with the way that wasn't as efficient but a habit. I get that...I stir things up in people. But whether that's good or bad is up to the beholder. I'm not saying anyone's inferior to me because I have high standards and great ideas. If you feel inferior, that's yours to heal and address...that's none of my business. But if I am in a state of consciousness of kindness, of holding the light, being the light, being myself and offering a set of standards to live by that are working, that helps humanity keep ourselves in check, keep order and harmony on the planet...I'm simply a messenger following my call. If you think I'm being superior, you're missing *your* call (to Truth, Intuition, Awareness). Check yourself before you wreck yourself.

Whenever the wrong point of view comes up, ask yourself: "What's coming up for me right now?" That's your homework assignment in that moment. Another assignment I have for the aware folks is- Just because you're aware of their high vibe, it doesn't mean that they think they're better than anyone. If you're aware that someone has a higher vibration than you, don't try to squash them down- Rise up. If you're aware that someone has high standards, don't feel offended as if they're trying to make you match them. It sounds like something in you is calling you to do and be something greater or try something new and you're resisting. The shortest way I can put that is- Stop shooting the messenger, for God's sake! If something starts stirring up in you when you meet somebody or are around somebody, you need to go within, take it to the mat and stop projecting it onto other people as if it's their problem. Because frankly, I'm tired of being on the receiving end of other people's blame. If I'm doing healing sessions, then that's something different. Let's take it into a session, open it up and look at it. Otherwise, projecting that your problem is my fault...this is not kind and I didn't ask for it. When I say this from the first-person perspective, I'm speaking on behalf of every other person who has had these experiences as well. They didn't ask for it, either. Stop trying to chop down the tallest tree. Learn from them. See from their advantage. Ask questions, stay open, but don't use them.

Haven't you realized that you tend to witness something <u>outside of you before you see it delivered to you, through you, for you, as you?</u> **People are often asking, *"Wow, what else is possible?"* in terms of what else are we capable of as spiritually gifted beings having a human experience, but then because it didn't happen to them firsthand, through them, when it shows up outside of them as someone else's experience, they want to kill the messenger. That person is being the answer to their question, but they thought it should come through them as the answer. This is why we should not be getting jealous of others due to what we witness outside of us. When we see it in others, we are next to experience it *if we stay open to it*...but if we become jealous and judge it, <u>we are shutting the doors to become it.</u>**

Now, as far as standards go...yes, there is a match and there is dissonance. In dating, our standards would need to be overlapping to a larger degree than a friend in order to be a match to begin with, because you just can't get there from there. There's not a bridge big enough to bridge that gap between someone who lives aligned with a certain belief system or standard and someone who doesn't. That's oil and water. There are levels and there are leniencies depending on what kind of collaboration you're having with others. If I were to collaborate with someone professionally, I would say they need to be aligned with starting events on time because otherwise it's not going to work. I am intentional, love details and order of an event as well as professionalism while some people like to show up last minute, and hesitantly start their event when someone suggests it. Those are dissonances in standards and you have to know what works for you on a personal, professional and, romantic level, in order to collaborate with others.

I once dated a guy who did not know what a deal-breaker was. I was astonished. I mean, here he was in his late 30s asking and I don't judge people, but it blew my mind. I think I first heard that term when I was in middle school. A deal breaker is what would break the deal. Like not having enough in common with someone, that's a deal-breaker. I also would not like to collaborate professionally with someone who doesn't value starting on time. That's a deal-breaker. If one love partner wants a family but the other doesn't– deal-breaker...time to move on and find your alignment elsewhere. Usually, a person who does not know what a deal-breaker is, is a person who has little to no standards and few goals. Literally they'll take anything that shows up. Oftentimes it's a default set by the culture around them or their family or they simply didn't realize they had a choice. I mean, there's a healthy level of being happy-go-lucky, low expectation. But then there's a level that looks like it that is actually based on low-balling, unworthy feelings and low-achieving behaviors. Those are two different intentions that appear similar to each other, but neither one of them set standards for themselves. What they also have in common is usually they don't realize they have a choice that they can choose. If you don't have any standards, then what are you aiming for? These are questions of differences, not coming from a tone of judgment. When you ask clarifying questions, you see what you are and you see what you are not. You see what you have, and you see what you don't have. You start to see that there are more choices than the mind had defaulted itself to see...from here, you can begin to choose.

I will say that it has been a common theme in spiritual circles of people showing up late or being very lax with starting events on time. And I would like to propose a question- Are you resisting and reacting to "The Man?" Some people are so anti-corporate and in a flow of "resisting the man" that they think it's OK to disrespect time. I don't agree with that because time helps things flow. Time creates order on the planet. Time creates quality and value. You can have an organized event be captured into this preconceived expected time frame of an hour, or you can have no organization, stretch it out to five hours, people feel totally watered down and drained because they were there so long and it took so long and they didn't know how long it would take before it would start or end and when and what are we doing next... there's just a lot of variables for an event that's undefined and this can incite anxiety, not freedom. If you would like to hang out, be undefined, say we're hanging out. But if you're creating an event, be organized, start on time. Have a cut-off time for starting on time.

Know what your rules are and share them...Are you letting late people in or are the doors closed on time? Some events do not permit late entry because it disrupts the energy of the entire room and the energy flow of the event. Once the event starts, the intentions are made, and now you're adding new energies to the room which are not on board because they didn't hear what was said before. And so the invocation gets skewed because the late people were not on board. This is crucial for healing circles who have a Code of Ethics like- *"What's said here stays here"*...trust circles are not fully cohesive due to the disrupted energy of late attendees. There's value to being on time. There's value to starting on time. And if you're secretly resisting and reacting to an invisible "the man", an institution or a government idea of authority on autopilot and don't realize it, you might want to see if that's still working for you. That resistance can help drive a person to start their own business at first, because you don't want to be part of some corporate culture out there. You don't want to be normal...you don't feel normal so you resonate with something different. You resonate with being an entrepreneur or doing something esoteric, teaching ancient sciences, mystery schools and mystical experiences or whatever you're bringing forth. That resistance is necessary to be a catalyst for change. But just be sure it's not running on autopilot where it doesn't need to be. We have to put the bridle on the horse to lead it to where we'd like to go. And as you're breaking your way through your business, you're deciding where it's going and you're deciding what energy is driving it. You hold the reins. Remember that. Those who resist authority cannot *be* authority.

Part 2

13

START WHERE YOU ARE & WORK WATCHA GOT

Start where you are & work watcha got. One thing that prevents people from answering The Call is they think that they're not enough or they don't have what it takes. I have a motto that'll get you going- Start where you are & work watcha got. I have lived this experience my entire life. You don't wait until everything is perfect to begin. And if you're waiting for perfection, you'll never start. Perfection is a self-fulfilling loop that runs on autopilot and hangs you up in it. You don't get anything done…you just remain in stasis, hanging from a tree.

The Call is innate. It's a natural urge. It comes from the Divine. It comes from breath, the same Energy Being that breathes you, gives you the desire and the dreams in your heart. And it's not something that's so far-fetched that you have to do a whole lot of things in order to be ready. It usually comes when you are ready. And if you look around you, you can start to count your resources, what's tangible to you, what's required for the first step. Is there something I need to learn that's required in order to get started? Who's in my network, in my circle that can contribute to this? Where can I launch this from? Is this a remote-only opportunity or is this in person? What community events can I attend to start getting myself seen for this?

These days you don't need to pay for a website. You can create a free page or a group for it on social media to get started as well as create an online profile similar to sharing a digital business card, but there are free variations of it where you can put an intro of yourself, share it by a QR code and get booking business started from there. It can cost $0.00 to start a business these days, although you won't have a business license and you will need to get legal at some point. Some people end up testing the waters without getting all the official things done first. If one is doing business unofficially from "stick it to the man" intent of evading paying taxes, they're also creating an energetic limitation on their manifestation. Anytime we try to create by resisting, the manifestation has crossed currents running through it. We want to create more, we'd like more money, we'd like more abundance but then we're also trying to run away from, not get too big, be invisible, hide from paying taxes. So those are two different streams of energies and they conflict with each other, sometimes cancelling each other out. When energy cancels each other out, things come to a halt or a standstill or they spin their wheels in the same direction going nowhere. When you remove the fear of paying taxes, and insert the knowledge of implementing legal tax loopholes, you can keep more of your money plus being wise with your money, creating longevity for your business and generational wealth.

Tax Evasion = Illegal; Tax Avoidance = Legal

In past times, we have been bullied to think that all tax loopholes are illegal because they must be illegal...where's the catch because there would not be so many easy ways to save money and keep more money in our pockets and not have to pay taxes on it. But in all actuality, these implications were projected at us to try and keep us small and in the dark so that we would pay more taxes and live poorly. While I do not claim to be an expert on taxes and their legal loopholes, be mindful of where you are educating yourself so you can have your life in order and prospering.

Millionaires and billionaires have been taking advantage of this knowledge for years while building generational wealth. It boils down to staying organized. If you stay organized, you'll feel more confident. And if you feel more confident, then everything will flow better, knowing that everything you're doing is legal and correct. What makes me more confident is creating a system to keep me organized. You have to create a system that works for you. How are you saving your receipts and how are you organizing your purchases? Some people use software and some people track them by hand themselves. I love the idea of Start where you are & work watcha got because it reinforces your natural abilities that first of all you are enough as you are. Second of all, your human experience here has cultivated skillsets that have not been put into action at your day job plus there are needs asking to be filled by humanity. These days, the job market is not sustainable as it is. It is very unreliable, especially with AI creeping up on us. Everyone needs to have a side gig that can have one, and I believe everybody can have one. You just have to know what what it is for you- what's fun for you or stimulates you that doesn't feel like work but you can make money doing it while helping others. Maybe you want to get into investments so that you don't have to like to create crafts and be creating stuff.

With education being in the palm of our hands these days, it's easier to get credentials and education from your home space than ever before. However, there have been a lot of layoffs these days with AI moving forward so there's a lot of highly educated people competing with each other in the job market. This may sound frightening, but I am speaking what's valid and truly going on right now and it stirs hearts to get real and clear about what you really love doing and where you are pivoting towards next. You may not need to invest in more education in order to be seen by someone hiring out there. You may have everything you need inside you to start where you are right now, being yourself, making a positive impact and making sure you are seen and heard, especially if you have lived the challenges of people not getting where you're coming from, making assumptions that are wrong and are in dire need of expanding their consciousness in order to evolve. What sets you apart from others? What sets people apart is who we are and what we have- our human experience, our skill sets, the things we're born with, the things we learn along the way, our life experience, the credentials we have. What gives us an edge up, is the spiritual side- How many lifetimes have I lived? What is the wisdom that we've experienced from those times and how can they benefit us here?

I once tried a new spiritual process, or at least "new" to me in this life, and long after I wasn't a newbie to it anymore, some of the people who introduced it to me, still projected onto me as if they are the expert and they are so much further along than I and they know everything about it and I'm still new. This is what I would call being an Absolute Expert. An **Absolute Expert may be knowledgeable about something but a dark element overlays their expertise in attempts to dominate others, squashing them out of channeling their own wisdom**...not human opinions or ideas, but True Divine Insight on the process/experience. It's great to have a Calling and I'm thankful they found a lifeline with the practice, but this type of person needs to pull their energy back to their field and stop trying to dominate others as if they hold no value. Ever stop doing what you love and not know why? Did someone overreach? Sometimes a person can project their energy too far into another's world, causing them to feel like they can't do that practice without them or at all any more. Months after I moved, I realized I'd stopped doing this practice because this person's domineering energy was attached to my supplies. I had to clear and reframe my field in order to remove their erroneous overreached energy out of my world.

    What these folks weren't able to see is that by the third time I participated in this practice, when I looked down to light the fire, instead of seeing my hands, I saw the tan hands of a male from another lifetime. It was the first lifetime that I had experienced this spiritual practice- I was a male at the time. Anytime I have had this type of experience, what's occurring is I'm tapping into the wisdom of that lifetime and bringing it to the present here. Since I allow this experience of merging that past consciousness with my current consciousness, I grow in leaps and bounds. This is how I surpass those who show me a practice in this lifetime. This has been my method for anything I learn in life. I am open to connecting the dots from previous lifetimes, picking up where I left off and soaring from there. Rarely do I learn anything for the first time in this lifetime unless it was invented in this lifetime (I am not a new soul). Whether or not you have the intuitive ability to see someone as they are, it's important that we don't make assumptions that we are the expert of the thing and that we don't project onto other people that they are less aware, that they are less experienced than us. **We need to be willing to see when someone's starting point in this lifetime is actually just a point of picking up where they left off in another lifetime.** When they start channeling in other things that are true about the method you thought you were the expert in, don't gaslight them out of their wisdom either. They hold the key to more information. And there's a reason why it reconnected in this lifetime.

    When a person pushes their energy in a way that dominates and infiltrates another person's world, this is overcompensation for something else not addressed. If this habit came from childhood, it is true that **those who are controlled will seek to control**. It could be that a person like this grew up in an environment where the elders were controlling and very little choice was allowed by the child but as an adult, you're not in that environment anymore of an elder being too controlling. Another way it could stem from childhood is if a child is not given proper boundaries and they're allowed to make all the choices and boss everyone else around, including the adults, overriding other people's Free Will. While letting the child make all the decisions can seem like a supportive, empowering thing to do, it gives them the message that other people don't have as good ideas as they have and they expect to get their way all the time. This person could grow up to be an adult who can't flow with life's changes that are outside of their control. No matter which environment created the byproduct of this massive energy push into other people's worlds, we all need to take a look at what we're doing with our energy and how we're being with others to keep harmony in our worlds and give others their rightful space. **Seek balance within, is all.**

Once when I had a money block, I went into a mild hypnosis by a practitioner and found that there was a lifetime where I was very poor *shoemaker* and struggled. Even though in that life, I made high quality shoes and was sought after by wealthy people willing to buy my merchandise, the struggle was still apparent. If you think about it as science states- past, present and future exists simultaneously. Theoretically, we can be experiencing a bleed-through from a previous lifetime impacting us in this lifetime and that's why we want to clear karma as much as possible and not create more of it in this life either. Otherwise, we're binding ourselves to this planet to keep reincarnating lifetime after lifetime. If you're born into a family belief system that there is only one life, that can be challenging because some people don't think that what they do has an impact...it doesn't matter, it's just this moment or life. If you took a broader point of view, you'd understood how it impacts you, not just linear moving forward, but in all aspects...then you would be a little more conscious and aware about your actions and inactions.

When we were able to see that this particular lifetime impacted me negatively in this lifetime, I was able to start working on those energies, reframing mental stories and emotional feelings. I hear the skeptic asking, *"How do you know this worked?"* A month after this session, I was entered into a raffle at work and I did not win. But the woman who won, her last name was **Shoemaker**. It was like the universal wink from God saying, *"Yes, we're listening and this is a confirmation that you're on track, you're working on this energy. This is why you didn't win."* A year later I did actually win two raffles, but this was long after doing the mental and emotional work it took to be new inside and attract a different reality...or align with the reality of winning. Once you dive into spirituality and see that there's more than just this one life that we're living, you see how deep it really is and how rewarding it is to dive deeper because you can adjust something in the past and it impacts you in the present. I can also play the devil's advocate here... even if there are no multiple lifetimes and maybe this story and imagery revealed in my subconscious mind during hypnosis to show me and illustrate a story of my inner world's climate so that I would know how to address it, then that's also a possibility. The fact that the lady's name was Shoemaker to corroborate this story would then be a demonstration that God is very much alive, flowing through all things and speaking to us, if we pay attention. I don't think it is wise to get stuck in one concept of spirituality or reality versus another, because usually when we believe something wholeheartedly without being open to other possibilities, that's where blind spot shows up, and then we have to detox from cognitive dissonance all over again.

FOG-RELEASE MEDITATION TECHNIQUE:

We can consciously go into a meditation and ask to be revealed an enhancement that enables our success. Close your eyes and get clear. If it helps, you can turn on music, but it's not necessary. It just depends on where your mind is. If the mind needs it, then put it on. If the mind is a little busy, then focus on the affirmation and intention: **"I am a clear and open channel for my higher self. Only God is allowed here advising me aligned with Divine Order. Thank you."**

Now what can show up? What you're asking for is that it's coming from God, but it might show up in different forms. It might show up as an Archangel speaking to you. Or you might feel it as an Ascended Master Presence like Jesus Christ, St. Germaine or Mary Magdeline.

As you get into that clear space, imagine what your inner sanctuary feels and looks like inside...this is the sacred space where you meet with God or your Aligned Guide for advice. How's your vision...are feelings or sight blocked? Tune into the areas that aren't clear and invite God to: **"Make easy and clear the way for my clear connection to God inside."**

Once it shows up, then you know you're in a safe location and ask: **"What spiritual qualities or gifts from former lifetimes can assist me right now in my journey with this challenge that I'm having?"** (you also may want to mention the actual challenge in detail...I am generalizing as a demonstration). Sit here until you start hearing something, seeing something, feeling something. You might find that you already had the epiphany before on what to do next, but right now you're feeling the reinforcement of that idea, or that idea is being expanded upon and broken down into further steps, pieces and ideas.

Take the time to breathe through any urge to dismiss it. Acknowledge any resistant or avoidant urges that may have tensed up your body. Do you feel rebellion in your body...why would we wish to rebel against God? If we are born of God, in God's image, this feeling/energy is not of God. Surrender it. If you're choosing to align with God's call, then everything

The Call

that is not God must leave right away with ease, please. Thank you.

Focus on this Affirmation: **"I surrender all self-dismissing, self-gaslighting habits, rebellious energies and feelings to the Christ Consciousness so that I AM free as a Sovereign Being to express and follow through on God's Call."**

Within this affirmation invocation, allow yourself to visualize these resistant energies, thoughts and feelings leaving you like fog rising off of your body and going into a light that's hovering above you. Everything that is not God is releasing off. You hardly feel fog when you're in the midst of it, unless you're in the midst of a rolling sea fog on the beach, because those can be pretty wet...you'll be drenched after getting caught in one of those, and those seem supernatural. What kind of fog is leaving you? A Sea fog, wet and heavy? Or light and airy? It's going away because it has kept you in the dark for too long and it doesn't need to be here. Who knows what it is and where it came from, and you don't need to know. You can go into this experience deeper if you like, but right now our intention is to start where you are & work watcha got and we're aiming to get there as quick as possible.

Start where you Are
& Work watcha Got.

14
You Can't Get there from there

    There is a spiritual world occurring right now through all of life, just as prevalent as there is a physical world. Just because you can't see it, doesn't mean it's not there, doesn't mean it's not affecting you. I know this firsthand from all the many paranormal experiences I've had and issues with energy awareness. I'd be feeling zen and peaceful, excited about meeting other people in social circles who also enjoy yoga, meditation or another spiritual practice. As soon as I walked into someone's aura, I picked up on their energy about me and if they didn't like me then I would end up acting like *I* didn't like *them* and suddenly a new stream of thoughtforms was expressing through me that wasn't even *mine. I* didn't have any negative thoughts about them before I walked up and suddenly it looked like I always did. This was highly frustrating because I would leave the occurrence saying, *"OMG Where did that come from? I don't even think that about them."* But it was what they secretly harbored about me. They thought that I thought negative things about them, or they simply had negative feelings and thoughts about me and I was too open so basically this stream of energy used me like a puppet to make me look bad. I found this to be a common occurrence in groups where a small amount of people were being control freaks, desperately clinging to being seen as the leaders and didn't want to make any room for me to come in and share the limelight even though what was going on at the time was not working and was dismantling on its own. They may have been asking the universe for the solution, but they didn't recognize it when it walked up and they tried to kill it before it had a chance.
    I have also noticed this occur when I have commented on someone's thread in a chat group. Immediately upon beginning to comment, a new stream of energy would commandeer my mind and say things that I did not even intend on saying, but it was because it was the intent of the

originator of that conversation or the group. **When your core purpose is to help build community and expand consciousness but you're made to look like you're anti-community and a menace to society**, it's highly frustrating to the point of me publishing this weird thing that's been happening to me, risking being hire-able ever again. But I feel like it's a phenomenon affecting way more people than just me, so we just need to get it out in the open and deal with it. After all, how many people has management fired, not because employees did something wrong, but because employees happened to be psychic, mirroring back the issues that management are creating? Are we willing to see the mirror?

Have you been willing to see yourself? Not as you think you are, but as you actually are, no matter how weird the answer may reveal to be. After all, can you be you if you're being all of these other people's energies? How can you get what you love if you're also attracting what is in alignment with all these other energies in your tow? I feel like many empathic people are having these experiences as well. Although it may not be true for every empathic or psychic person, it's a specific experience for some people. Is the law of attraction not working out for you because you didn't realize these other energies were attached to you or infiltrating you from other sources?

I've been watching this energy pattern since I was a kid, where someone near me was psychic enough to intuit what I was about to do and they acted like it was their idea, doing it first, which caused me to look like the copycat when actually they were picking this out of my field psychically. It wasn't their idea – they were aware of it in me. This influence didn't stop there – it would gaslight me through me as well, causing me to expose my own content's punch lines before I had the chance to get published with them myself. Meanwhile, some people assumed that I was a gaslighter...but what they didn't realize was they were picking up on the entity or energy of gaslighting...not that I personally partake in it, but that it was in my field as a presence. Some people thought the same thing about me when they perceived an "affair" energy in my field. I do not participate in marital affairs nor any kind of affairs with people who are not single. If you perceive an energy in someone's field, be sure you don't spread rumors about them that this is the thing they do. Clarify whether this is an entity or an energy that you're picking up on, and seek counsel within to find their true intentions. It took a long time for me to get that affair entity out of my field, and it showed up at the most inopportune times to block the progress that I could make with my spiritual career. Of course, that is

The Call

common for a gaslighting element, an element that wants to stop you before you have a chance to make a positive impact.

"You can't get there from there" - that was said by Abraham Hicks. Part of receiving your dreams begins as you notice what energy you are being then aligning your body and your mind to feel the way you would feel after already having the thing that you were aiming to manifest. One narcissistic personality I ran into in the wellness industry wanted me to write for their business. I made it clear and verbalized it that I'm not a ghostwriter, but I'll be happy to contribute from my perspective and get credit for my perspective because I knew, although I'm not a published author yet, I will be and I deserve to be recognized for my contributions. This is someone who had repeatedly sought my counsel over the years for his personal life and business, so he knew I have a unique energetic perspective to speak from. Even though I was clear, I guess he was so focused on his goals he thought he would just get away with whatever he wanted to, regardless of what I was saying. It's bad when somebody does that to you, but it's even worse when they're considered to be a friend. Either they're an unwell friend, or they never were your friend altogether and had a secret agenda against everyone and only for them, so that they can achieve their goals in spite of and because of everyone. **This is what I would call being <u>Minionized-</u> It's when they see your value enough to use you for their benefit, but they don't want to give credit where it's due. They want to make you their minion while receiving all the glory and praise for your perspective and contributions. No one deserves to be minionized.** This person thought that they could continue stealing from me and others around, yet they were mystified at why their business kept breaking down every few years by their employee leaving suddenly. Greed and laziness was their upper-limiting problem, and if they're still having that problem, they're most likely still stealing.

I have noticed that some people's health and wealth problems never change…these same people are ones that stole from others. I once met a guy and soon after, he suddenly shared with me his whole Google Drive full of content that he had bought over the years…books, webinars, etc. from different creators. I was alarmed at how much he was sharing with me because we didn't even have a conversation about him sharing anything. It was just an automatic default that he would go into, I suppose, when meeting someone new. I was slightly flattered at the kind thought of inclusion and support but also alarmed as a creator. I knew in the future I would definitely be published and have works to sell digitally and I don't feel right about sharing other people's stuff without paying.

This person also was in the midst of a divorce that had been going on for years, to no resolve, over land and money. While inclusion and support were a kind gesture, what you steal from others will be taken from you as well, even if in another way. Share creators' purchase links...not their downloads.

Everyone deserves respect...everyone deserves credit where due. Everyone's perspective is unique. And if you are stealing from somebody, you're borrowing time. You're borrowing energy and essences. You're harvesting someone's soul and you're expressing a perspective that's not yours. If you've already done it and you're still reaping the reward, it's up to you and God within to make amends, right the wrongs or keep barely getting by.

Years ago, I was approached by someone I trusted and they started asking me questions about a topic. As I answered, I wasn't pulling from my human mind space of things I learned in this life...I was channeling in the actual Truth which extended beyond my human capacity...these were realizations of deeper meanings of the Bible that other people had not been noticing but I had been since I was a teen and I planned on writing a book about it. I thought we were just having spiritual conversations and enjoying expanding our consciousness. But after a few weeks, this person announced that they were writing a book and it included the very topic and answers that I had given them. If I had known they were pumping me for answers that they would profit off in a book, I never would have answered their questions. I would have turned them away saying, *"Go within, all your answers are within."* and if they lost interest in the idea altogether over time due to no answers revealing, they would've realized it wasn't theirs to bring forth...that they were aware of my book that I was going to write and they thought it was theirs. If this was their book to bring forth, they would have had the answers within them. They wouldn't have had to tap me for them. **If you're using other people as a Clear Channel to help you write, you might want to think about whether this is your content to bring forth, or if you should rise up and be the mentor that the next step in your evolution is calling you to be by encouraging others to bring forth their projects that your awareness is perceiving in them.** Some people use the oneness concept in a dark way, thinking- *"We're all one, so all knowledge is mine to use whether it comes through this person versus me."* while they also use the forgiveness idea as a permission slip to do whatever they want to do at the others' expense (*I'll just Ho'oponopono it later*).

Similarly, in these types of energy dynamics, I've seen that usually their problems don't go away until they *do* come clean. Coming clean doesn't always look clean. You might lose everything. But you can gain your health, wealth and right relationships...there's a lot of reward in doing that. They might have a whole new set of followers, but this will be more authentic to who they truly are because it's not on borrowed energy from others. When we borrow energy from others, we're riding their coattails. In the legal world, if someone were to come clean, they would also have to turn over the legal rights of the works that were stolen and offer proceeds percentages to the person from past sales. Some people think that because it's spiritual work, it's not really *real* work. There's a little bit of a gaslighting dismissive quality to it, so they don't think they need to get legal involved or start reimbursing the real source of the work. But that dismissive gaslighting energy is not of the light of God. There's nothing Godly about that energy. And God is a God of Divine Order, and I think that Divine Order would ask for this energy to be cleared and for the original content creator to be revered.

How much of your following have you built on others' stuff? What is original to you? People who take from other people will constantly be looking for more content because they're not learning from within, so they're going to run out and they're scared to run out because they know it's not theirs and they're freaking out looking all around them horizontally instead of looking within them vertically. This chapter may sound heavy-handed, but it needs to be addressed...no one else has. When you do the work, your own work produces...It's like gardening. You plant the seed. You nurture the soil with water and sun. You prevent pests from coming in with natural pest-resistant plants. You trim where needed. Some people sing to or do energywork on their plants...and they produce eventually. It took time to build underneath.

Being an original creator takes: 1. The yearning to express something new and 2. Asking questions to the Universe, hearing the Divine within then 3. Taking aligned action. Since energy doesn't lie, the universe flows to you based on the energy you are. This is why people attract partners they don't like- something in them is a magnet for it, even if it's not their own energy as I have seen in my own world. Some Lightworkers chuckled and mocked me behind my back, thinking that I didn't notice why was attracting guys with "Peter Pan Syndrome"...they thought it was because I was being that energy and not seeing my blindspot. It was actually something deeper going on- being too open to the collective energy in that city while the dominant vibe in that city for people my age was Peter Pan Syndrome. Many people had it, male and female. It was a vacation/retirement culture city and a lot of people just wanted to party and have fun and almost no one my age had retirement accounts on the radar. What if many of these people are simply too open to other people's energies and have soaked up the culture around them? Can you serve the vacationers and retirees without becoming a vacation-retired mentality, meeting lucrative and responsible goals? It's tough to be in it and not of it. Don't mistake my honesty for a lack of compassion. We have to see where we are to enable us to get to where we aim. **If it stings, it rings. Embrace the pings as Truth only hurts when we are either misaligned with it or had not been willing to see it before.**

15

Hindsight is 20/20....
Foresight is 20/15

Hindsight is 20/20...but foresight is 20/15...When I had lasik eye surgery, they brought my vision up to 20/15 vision which is a little better than perfect. It was wonderful. Coming from being 20/2024, that space of needing to wear glasses to walk to the toilet in the middle of the night because all you see is color everywhere, you would not be able to see if you're going to step on anything...to seeing better than perfect, seeing details on leaves from 10 feet away that you never saw before...that's amazing. It was the best gift I ever gave myself in my 20s...I had been wearing glasses since 4th grade.

One thing I was not warned of when achieving your dreams is the spiritual world. You might make a positive step for yourself in the physical world like paying $3,000 for better-than-perfect eyesight...at a time where I made $2.13/hour plus tips serving...this was a major investment for me, a big leap I stretched to achieve for myself. But no one told me the negative would come after me. Within a couple of months after buying this expensive investment for myself, I was challenged by getting into this relationship with a functioning alcoholic. His high level of drinking caused me to drink more and alcohol's hard on your eyesight. Here I have just invested all this money into my eyesight and I'm still doing the drops (there were a sequence of drops for the eyes to help them adjust) but I was drinking heavier, not knowing why. I was embodying his energy, having no awareness that I was wide open. This was long ago, before I was deep into this healing work and reading the energy flows of life. Had I been aware, I wouldn't have involved myself with him at all. We were pitted together by others' manipulative energy flows and I had no clue. It was energetic. It wasn't physically in front of my face. The signs were there, pointing to leave him...I ignored the yellow flags and the red flags then ended up moving out with him where there was a Black Flag- I could have died. Even then, in my primitive aware spaces, I knew that I had a choice and I looked myself in the mirror and said, *"No matter what, I choose to come out of this alive."* It was that split second intention I made with myself in the mirror that kept me alive. I don't want to go into that right now. It's a interesting story with lots of synchronistic signs and symbols. But you don't want a Black Flag.

Some of us got a Black Flag because it jarred us into an awakened experience. I knew from then on this was absolutely my choice and I made the wrong choice by getting into this relationship. By then I could see clearly how I was manipulated into it by energies of other people around me. And how the universe gave me a green flag with someone new early in this relationship and I could have gone a different direction with a different partner, but I didn't choose him. This choice of getting the Black Flag led me on this trajectory I'm on today. So why wait for Hindsight's 20/20 when you can use Foresight's 20/15? **Foresight's 20/15 Definition is- Psychic skills, Intuition...Don't miss the flags. Even if you don't know what they mean or why- Slow down, Stop. Be present. Shift trajectory.** It's the times that I did not slow down, that I didn't ask why, that I didn't stop, that I didn't be present, that I didn't make a different choice, even though I had a feeling I should...that impacted many people's lives. It went the wrong way, when it could have been better. While I don't engage in acts that lack integrity like stealing, cheating, or illegal acts, I have often looked guilty because I was unwilling to see how dark the people were around me. **Do not risk your life.** As they say, don't tempt fate. Think of that next time you're trying to get your amazing selfie. There's been enough cautionary tales of folks raising the stakes too high just for one pic, one last pic. Was it worth it? Those left behind mourning the loss won't agree.

Growing up in Christianity, I always heard, *"Draw near to God and He will draw near to you."* Another way to say it is, *"What you seek is seeking you."* If you're asking for the truth, you'll get it. But you need to be willing to receive the answer, no matter what kind of answer it is. This is part of being a Seer. See in the future. As I like to say, *"Peering down a portal."* Anytime you meet somebody, you're crossing paths and you can peer down the portal to see what that life would be like with them or what the outcome is in a scenario. No matter how many yellow, red, and black flags we may ignore, you can't change a person's spots. They are who they are.

Please believe them when they tell you and show you who they are. And then walk away.

AFFIRMATIONS AND PRAYERS:

"My words are charged with prospering power. All that has offended me, I forgive. Within and without, I forgive. Things past, things present, things future, I forgive. I forgive everything and everybody who can possibly need my forgiveness of the past and present. I forgive positively everyone. I am free and they are free too. All things are cleared up between us now and forever." – Catherine Ponder

"I'm sorry. I love you. Please forgive me. Thank you." – Ho'oponopono

"Our Father, who art in heaven, hallowed be thy name; Thy kingdom come; Thy will be done, on Earth as it is in Heaven. Give us this day, our daily bread; And forgive us our debts, as we forgive our debtors; Leave us not in temptation, but deliver us from evil. For thine is the kingdom, and the power, and the glory, forever. Amen." – The LORD's Prayer

"Then Jesus said, 'Father, forgive them, for they know not what they do.' " – Luke 23:34

"I call on the law of forgiveness. I am free from mistakes and the consequences of mistakes. I am under grace and not under karmic law." – Florence Scovel Shinn

"God, please take this from me. Of myself, I can do nothing. "

"Make easy and clear the way."

SONGS:
"Let There Be Peace On Earth" – Sy Miller
"Across The Universe" – The Beatles

16

WHEN WE KNOW BETTER, WE DO BETTER

"We're always doing the best we can given the knowledge, the understanding and the awareness we have in each moment." – Louise L. Hay. I read this quote for the first time in 2012 in her book "You Can Heal Your Life" but the first time I heard that quote was actually before 2002 when I was staring at myself in the mirror and talking to God. This is back in the day where we couldn't just Google anything. There was no smart search engine. You had to climb through page after page of online search results on AskJeeves...there were no optimized searches. Everything was just online *some*where. Keywords didn't bring up much. We relied heavily on dictionaries and encyclopedias because not much was on TV then either...we didn't have all the channels we have today. We didn't have apps. Streaming didn't exist. If you wanted to know anything, you had to **Meditate. Go within. Ask God, Look in the mirror.** That's it. I didn't even know what the word meditate really meant. I saw it in the Bible once and then when I was at school I found an encyclopedia that elaborated on it. But I didn't really know what meditation was. I had spontaneous moments of losing all thought, hearing deafening silence, seeing visuals. And then I thought, well, maybe that's what it is. I found my body doing a lot of yogic things that later on, turned out to be part of kundalini training and consciousness expansion. But at the time I was Baptist, so I was just doing what my body wanted to with breathwork and poses. When I finally got my own bedroom again in middle school, I sat in silence a lot and found solace in God and advice from beyond. When Louise's quote came to me in the mirror, I think was God answering a question to help me feel better about some of the chaos going on in my life at the time.

Lack of awareness from others can be negligence but it's not intended negligence because lack of awareness just is where the person is at the time until they learn better. I would sum this up as *"When we know*

The Call

better, we do better". It is usually only the heart and ego that refuses to do better after we have already learned better. A real reform, not one where they fake it and then commit more evil...a real reform is inspiring and can spread personal growth in a community like wildfire. When we know better, we do better. But often the program, the parasitic program humans have, is judgment first. When you judge, you cut off awareness. To be aware is to expand, having a broad sight, spreading your wings to cease alignment with the familiar so that Truth is not missed. To judge is like clipping others' wings, and even your own, since it requires contraction in order to align with judgment. In times that I was made to look guilty by evil, my friend circles judged, and dispersed, assuming I was a part of the ill deeds. No one was mature enough to address it head on, ask questions, and talk it out. If they had, we'd probably still be friends hanging out today. After all, *"what kind of person could think that I would do such a thing"* is what I was often left with. We have an immature society and what tends to happen is people skirt the issue. They crave the leadership positions for prestige, money and social status but shrink back from responsibility, make passive-aggressive jokes, half hug you, give the illusion of community while actually being a clique that you're not a part of, and once the veil drops, you don't really want to be there anyway, since their integrity and reverence to service is a front. (*Yikes, can you close the curtain now? Lol*)

Can we have better conversation skills than our forefathers, our teachers, and parents? And can we ask questions without condescending or accusatory tones? Can we resolve matters without assumptions, without assuming the worst about people and dividing them out of communities erroneously. **Gray areas can be tough to navigate in a community but after a fall-out, if your idol has fallen, the side YOU take exposes who YOU are.**

There's nothing said in secret. To a psychic, everything is heard. But people forget even a psychic can have a blind spot. If they weren't willing to see the darkness in one person, they had that one blindspot. Judgment jeers, *"How are they psychic and they didn't see this?"* Well, you know, at least they answered The Call. They knew they had a gift of being psychic and they started doing readings or whatever, and then something happened outside of their purview and it was a learning experience. If drama goes down, we ought to be spreading our wings and holding space for people, even if we're not a fan of those who are affected. They're learning in their worlds as well, and when we judge, we will certainly be judged. How we treat others is the way of being that we are impressing upon the formless universe, and that is a message telling the universe that that is how we would like to be treated. There's a lot of messages going out from you that are non-verbal and you may not have connected those dots before, but I think the Bible said it quite clearly and metaphysically- *"Judge not, lest you be judged."* Another way to say it is- *"What goes around, comes around."* The more we begin to take the higher road and hold space for others instead of judging, the more we will have others doing that same thing to us as well. And then our manifestations will get clearer and better with ease.

REFRAMING MEDITATION TECHNIQUE

Take a moment and set this intention: **"I am open, ready, and willing to receive new insights with grace and ease about people and situations that are in alignment for me to perceive at this time. Thank you."** With your eyes closed, let this be your meditation and be willing to receive epiphanies that could be wildly opposite to what you thought was true or confirmations of what you already knew. If we believe in untrue narratives, we are living a façade. Façades are like a house of cards you live in…you don't hold the matches but you will get burned later. Wouldn't you rather face it now and have control over your options?

What I'm praying to invoke here is the liberation of the innocent from being viewed in a skewed light. It's a heavy burden to bear, especially for sensitive, empathic people. My intention is also to expand consciousness, so if we know what to look for, we can ask better questions to Consciousness/God and act differently moving forward since the way humanity has been moving before is not working anymore.

17

Enough is Enough

Enough is enough. Sometimes you gotta have that stance with the universe. I mean, how many times do we allow a certain pattern to go forth over and over without shifting something? Is everyone meant to write a book about their pattern? Not really. They find other ways to shift their reality. But this is the way that I feel is appropriate for me. When I was 10 years old or so, I was playing Barbies with my sister, and suddenly I caught a vision. I didn't know what a vision was, but I knew I wasn't asleep. Usually you only dream when you're asleep...I was awake so this is a vision. I had heard of visions in the Bible before where several characters had dreams and visions, but this was a vision of me sitting at a table signing books and I had the knowing that I wrote those books. I was like, *"Ohhhhh."* I felt this brilliant, empowering energy around it and I knew that I would be a published author. The vision appeared as a revelation of what my future path held. Maybe everyone is not meant to share their stories as a published author, but I knew in that moment, this was my destiny. It wasn't a default that I settled into simply because self-publishing options are so readily available to me in today's time. I thoughtfully considered this for many years before launching in public because I know once your anonymity is gone, there's no getting it back.

Since then, that idea has been on the back burner. I knew I would write something but I didn't know what. I was having paranormal experiences and I was thinking, *"Well, maybe I'll be writing about that."* I didn't know I'd be reading energy fields and watching these weird patterned manifestations come, having to combat people's energy intentions, moving their energy out of my field. I didn't know this was actually a spiritual warfare as it has been but as I've seen, people's energy intentions have been trying to infiltrate me, stop me from doing what I'm here to do as well as manipulate me for their personal gain. Some people have manipulating tactics...they need to clean up, stay in their own lane, stop trying to control other people and, instead, control their own inner worlds.

At some point in my 20s, I thought seriously about writing. Since then, I have gone through at least four computers. Each time I started a project, something would happen and the computer would die. So the project would die with it or was barely started. But it was just the idea of *"Ohh my gosh...every time I start this project, something goes wrong with the technology. What is this?"* I wasn't connecting the dots that the energy world is able to infiltrate technology as well, so I had to start beginning working with deeper intentions that encompassed everything. If God is omnipresent, so is the anti-God. It's the anti-consciousness lashing out. I started creating better intentions that protect God's work through me so that I can actually get things accomplished here. *"Enough is enough"* is a great line to draw. It's like, *"OK, I've seen this reality happen more than once. I'm done with it. Other people don't have this issue. Stop it!"*

We have the power to choose. We have the power to change. And the choice is ours to make. One day last year I asked my computer on a whim what its name was and it told me and I was like *"Ohh, I didn't expect that."* The weird things that show up...like I'm not trying to imagine a name, I'm not making up anything. I'm not sitting here with an overactive imagination. But the words came to me and I was like, *"Ohh, interesting."* This is an interaction between me and the universal field. I'm not trying to program myself into thinking that I'm hearing conversations from inanimate objects or even entities, but I do hear from entities at times. Sometimes you have to draw the lines with them too. I was once dating this guy and I had laid down to go to bed. I was thinking about how it wasn't working out with us because you can't get there from there.... I mean the gap was pretty big of differences between us, not enough overlap. And then I heard someone beam in with a female voice, *"Ohh give him a chance."* Immediately, I knew it was his deceased mom chiming in from the other side as a middleman, as a mediator. I thought *"Oh my God that's new. Now someone's crossed over loved one has come in as their hypeman."* As sweet of a notion as that was, and unexpected, there was not enough to keep us together and I have a choice here.

When we begin answering The Call, taking steps towards it, our programming comes up, so we need to recognize if we are experiencing something out of a struggle default programming and if that works for us moving forward. Being a conscious creator, and not just a consumer of what is showing up, we can decide, *"Hey, that's not working for me.*

Enough is enough. What would I rather have happen instead? I'd rather not be coerced by a being from beyond into a relationship that is not working for me, that only works for the other person. And I'd rather not be bullied by technology passive aggressively as I'm following through on steps that are aligned for me. God would not desire a struggle reality for me as I'm following through on my alignment. If I am struggling or struggle is coming up, that is the lens through which I am experiencing life that needs adjusting. And so I ask, what do I have to believe for this to be showing up this way?" And that's where things start to change. Get more fluid. And then I can get solid on the ideal outcome.

18

BE THE CHANGE YOU WISH TO SEE

Be the change you wish to see. It's such a common platitude in spirituality, and yet many people avoid it by all attempts. Being a change means being different. Some people would rather be the same, and they're looking for more of the same. Now, there is a line to notice and draw for your own safety and sanity...if you're the only one in a group of people who are being kind and respectful and they keep trying to steal from you or are jealous of you, or are attacking you then by all means, I'm not saying stay. You have to know when to cut your losses and let them grow at their slower pace while you continue to soar at yours. And I say slower because yes, if you're jealous of another person, or coveting, that is a low energy. If you are embodying that and you don't think that you are and you don't acknowledge that you are the problem, then you're really in the thick of that energy that needs healing and clearing. In that lower space, energy moves slower.

You have to be willing to be different in order to have what you love because everyone is different, whether you acknowledge it or not. The challenge is thinking that everyone is the same. We may have similar needs, but we are not the same. And if you think that you're the same, you might end up sticking yourself under another person's flow of energy. When you're under another person's flow of energy, it gets really frustrating because then you feel constipated, like you're not allowed to go do something. If you're feeling like you're not allowed to go do something, and you literally have all the freedom in the universe to go do it, you might want to look at where your energy is flowing and what is causing it to stop. You also need to be willing to see when you're outgrowing your teacher, mentor or person you follow online. If you're not willing to see that you're growing at a faster pace, or that your wisdom is asking to be heard by You within you then you're going to miss your growth moment, and inevitably, your Call. You're going to miss your evolution. And while it's nice to support great leaders out there...I'm hoping some people will enjoy this work here that I've learned from my wisdom, there's a natural ebb and flow of finding support in each other here or there as it feels aligned vs the self-reliance of going within. If you don't support yourself, you won't be growing within and then you'll go stagnant. To prevent stagnancy, we must be balancing: going within for solitude time to see what we're learning from our lives and to see if anything new is showing up vs going without to follow our favorite people, nurturing our friends' works, leaving room for new people to join in, not just established friend groups. While some people may have great ideas and they might have good direction for themselves, it might be that your inner guidance tells you something totally opposite and it doesn't mean what others suggest is bad, it just means that you need to develop the muscle to go within and trust your inner knowing more so than someone outside of you. One time someone invited me to attend a group and I responded to them, *"I go where I'm aligned."* And it made their head spin because how would I not feel aligned in that group? She didn't see that the person she saw as a leader was actually being backstabbing towards me. If you want to grow spiritually, you have to be willing to see the blind spots even in someone you put on a pedestal. If not, you're slowing your roll to be slower than theirs. You're putting yourself under their flow. You're capping your abilities.

If you want to be a freed being, you have to be willing to be different. Because while you might have people that you're a fan of, you also know that there's a possibility you'll surpass them and that there only is the glass ceiling you allow to be there. It may be challenging to outgrow somebody who meant a lot to you and showed you the way but what if they have challenges show up that block them from growing even further? Or what if they end up being jealous of someone and that stunts their growth? What if their intentions get skewed because of something they're healing? And what if they start digressing instead of expanding?

A free thinker has no problem cutting losses but the danger lies when people align and agree with everything a group of people says because if that group of people ends up skewing in a false direction incrementally over time, you won't be able to see that what they're resisting and reacting to is actually Divine Order showing up in a different form. Little by little, step by step, thought by thought, there was the habit of align and agree, align and agree, align and agree, and then you're walking in lockstep with each other as if you're chained physically to grow at the same pace when no one has set those limits on you...they happened over time, subconsciously and energetically...and usually innocently, right, because everyone wants to belong somewhere. If everyone's trying to feel good all the time and the message is about that, and if no one's creating the message about being different and growing beyond challenges, will you remember that being different isn't wrong? These things happen on autopilot, subconsciously...on accident. I'm not being mean and I'm not trying to cut down anyone's group, but you need to be able to recognize when a community stops being a community and it's actually become a clique...or worse than a clique, a cult. It's a slippery slope, and there's subtle differences between all of them but it happens subtly, step-by-step, over time. This is why a variety of messages needs to be brought to a community and everyone needs equal representation. To have a community, one must override their own ego to be the shining star. There is a period of creating routines in a community using the same strong leadership but strong leadership can recognize when other new folks have wisdom to teach and talents to share, rotating them in as well.

I once sat in a group and this person led us in Kirtan. Kirtan is Sanskrit music. It sounds really beautiful. Usually the facilitator explains what it means so that you know what you're singing. It's call and repeat where they sing a little bit and then we repeat that stanza... it's a back-and-forth thing. I think the closet thing it resemble is an alter call...I usually feel a reverent space while singing, if led by a Present facilitator. Unfortunately, the energy and intent of this person was kind of haughty. It was like her inner child showed up to perform, projecting petty, vindictive energy like- *"Nana Nana Boo Boo."* but meaner...more like- *"So there! I'm a singer too! I can play too! Listen to me, it's my turn!"* It was so rank with the stench of ego, I couldn't even find myself willing to sing with it. I fell into a deep compassion space for her embarrassing moment and focused on blocking that energy from entering my body by putting my hands in specific mudras. I went as neutral as possible. I didn't want to get any part of that energy in me. I felt really bad for her because I knew she would realize what she did right away. And I just wanted to bring a space of peace and full acceptance to her as she was in that moment rather than judgment and without projecting onto her, *"Hey, you know what you just did?"* So I focused on being neutral. And later on, as we parted ways, I gave her a hug but she almost didn't want to receive me because I knew in that moment, when I brought that space of full acceptance and compassion, she caught the awareness of how she represented herself. I wasn't judging her for it. I was embodying the space of compassion for her ego moment. Some people reading this might think that I'm having a moment of being superior, but honestly, I'm not. I'm showing what it's like to energetically, nonverbally, and without condescension, show people acceptance for even their worst ego moments. What people need most after that, is more space for them to see that they are loved as they are. I was ready to hear her talents that day and looking forward to it, but when the ego moment happened, it was just tainted and smeared. I could not do anything but what I did, which was protect myself and then shift into an accommodating space to give that energy within them the Presence of God that it needed to heal itself, to love itself back into oneness and wholeness. Ego moments like this happen when you haven't been seen or heard in a really long time and you've been hiding your talents. Who did it to you first? You did. You have to stand up for yourself and you have to put yourself in the limelight little by little, even if you start with a friend group. Start sharing with friends and then grow it into community to build your confidence.

It's never anybody else's fault outside of you that you've been hiding your light although you might need to look a little further to find places where you can shine it, if you're in a community of people who think the worst about you or find your light so bright that they feel inferior. That's not your fault either. We're told to shine our light and then we're cut down by people who say, *"Ohh no, not that bright."* So it seems that any time somebody has a mixed message like that, you have to be willing to stand up for yourself and get yourself the heck out of there, for one thing. But know when to stand up for yourself or when to just quietly back out because some groups like this can be pretty volatile and take time to grow to let you in. Any time you're shining your light and you get cut down, you need to expand. It is a sign that you have outgrown that area, those people, that venue, and something bigger is coming forward. So shine, never back down, never hide your light. And hold people accountable when it's appropriate.

Some people think that you're not good enough and that you're too much at the same time and you can't rewire a person like that...they have to work that out in their own consciousness because they don't make sense to their own self. They certainly wouldn't make sense to you if you tried to sort them out unless you're psychic and can give them a reading to see exactly what is going on. But as I have learned, most people do not want to be read. And if they do, you might as well have them sign a waiver first, because some of them, you know, try to shoot the messenger.

19

Follow-through & Circle-back

 Following through may be the achievement of a lifetime for some people...and that's great. We should celebrate our wins. Even if they seem small compared to others. Remember, we're not comparing ourselves to others, but following through on an initiative, a Higher Calling...It's a big deal to be struck by an idea that you feel the urge to address or solve for humanity, or it's doing something you love doing naturally...it's a beautiful thing. Follow your bliss.

 So why don't we follow through? Sometimes with technology being in the palm of our hands, we may feel a little overwhelmed by all the notifications pulling us in multiple directions at once, distracting us from a new routine we are creating. We make plans and then we don't uphold them, calling frequent cancellations "being in the flow with the universe". Then unkind trends go viral...like ghosting and you're aware of the collective ghosting culture energy and feel weird for going against the norm who ghost a lot even though you know it hurts people to not honor your word and show up for others. Yet, each time a person is ghosted, they trust less and less in that person and eventually their trust is eroded to believe that community is even possible. What we're training each other to believe by ghosting each other is that you can't depend on anyone and everyone's word means nothing while we all secretly crave real connection, support and deep friendships that extend beyond surface level. Things change when you follow through, and you have to be willing to move through changes without stopping dead in your tracks. We can't continue to do the same things and expect to get new results. In order to get something new, you have to do something different. To do something different means you must follow through...that is being the change. If you're having a physical symptom show up at the thought of or in the action of following through, people address that in different ways. Some people do breathwork, get on anxiety medication if it's needed, some people drink Kava (a relaxing herbal drink and non-habit forming) and some people drink alcohol or smoke cigarettes. There are many different ways and methods that people move through the resistant feelings in their body. I would never advise or prescribe anything because I'm not a doctor and I don't know what is best for you. Usually, people have tried one or the other, or a combination of what I mentioned and that journey is for you to realize by listening to your body.

What helps create a lasting change, though? Any of these can aid you in the moment when you're feeling anxiety but asking the question, *"What do I have to believe for this to be true?"*, can reveal the cause of the anxiety symptom. Perhaps there is a belief about not saying the right things or a fear of looking stupid while being asked hard questions and not knowing how to respond. If you could take one moment to address the thought or feeling that comes up when you ask this question, then you can start gaining traction and control over it. We don't need to have the right responses and it's OK to say, *"I don't know".* Or *"Let me give that some thought and let's talk about it next time."* When I have experienced anxiety, it was a symptom of a different cause and we can continue to address symptoms because we need to in the moment but this is a survival solution. It doesn't reach the deeper parts of us unless we start asking better questions, thinking introspectively about how we perceive ourselves and facing our fears of how others perceive us. This would be a thrival solution rather than survival and lasts long-term. What some people need are more conversational skills, and believe it or not, the conversation starts within first. If you don't know what's running your program, you don't know how you're showing up, and you don't know what you're avoiding that could be your dream life in disguise.

Some people think that life is random and chaotic and there's no connection to anything showing up. And yes, that can be true in some cases – it is synchronistic and has its mysteries, but this type of person would have more order if they would follow through and circle back. This is the type of person who makes all kinds of commitments, doesn't know what they're doing because they don't circle back and follow through. They might be an airy-fairy kind of person, ungrounded, unfocused or withdrawn and surrounded by energetic walls you can feel a mile away but it can be frustrating dealing with these types because you never seem to get anywhere with them or they're so nonchalant about plans they made, even if you're trying to give them business, they act like you're the inconvenience for confirming the time and the place. Or they promised to call with solidified plans, but their outreach never comes.

Instead, I see posted in a community thread that they are advertising that thing that they are selling me but where was their follow through and circle back to confirm a time with me when we had arranged plans for me to buy something from them? Even though I really was looking forward to buying the item from this person, I'm not working for her. He's working for me. If he's selling to me, he's working for me. He made a promise to call me with a confirmed time to exchange and he did not deliver. Even though it bums me out to not have that item that I was looking forward to having, I am done acting like everyone else's servant and personal assistant holding other people accountable for their word- it's not my job. Whenever it is aligned, then that item will come back around for the same good price or better because no item is worth chasing down at the cost of my respect. Clients and customers don't deserve being dismissed.

 I was once in a community thread and someone placed an introduction on there in attempts to meet people in town because they just moved into the area and wanted to connect. I replied, *"OH I'd love to connect."* Then there was no response. No reply, no personal DM, no acknowledgement at all. The next thing I see, they're promoting a workshop for business owners. This is a person who claims to be a business mentor...but where was their communication?

 Both of these occurrences are passive aggressive. It's like something withholding something from me. I realize I am the common denominator energetically, yet it doesn't explain why they are behaving that way. I see that I have attracted it. Do we see how we are being with other people? Are we reliable or are we flaky? Over and over I show up to make friends and meet new people with an open mind, knowing that this area is very diverse and they may not share all of my common points of view and then they show up flaking out and not following through. It makes for great content to write about, but I'd actually like to get somewhere with building community and not just be gaining content to sell as a reflection of others' behaviors.

 People who follow through make great employees. People who circle back make great employers. If you want to do the bare minimum, then get started and do nothing else. If you want to make a difference, then go above and beyond. We don't build community by making plans and forgetting what they are. We build community by seeing the value in others that we make plans with and respect them enough to show up for them. Even if you don't care about yourself, at least show up for other people. If you're self-dismissive, make sure you're not dismissing others. You don't know where they came from and what they're healing and these are often occurrences that make people not want to try and show up for others at all...because they're not being respected as a human. Sometimes things do happen out of our control and sometimes people overcommit, so they don't really remember all the arrangements they made. Maybe doing business through text threads doesn't work for them, but they haven't realized it or created a system that does work for them. It's in my nature to follow through and circle back, so I can't relate. This is simply speculation based on one occurrence per person and I don't know them very well. But I find it interesting that people claim to be a leader, have a business coaching entrepreneurs yet they are not following through and circling back when people reach out to connect with them. If you give it a minute, people will expose themselves. Just be sure you don't take it personally and keep your power intact because it's not about you. Some people have things they're working on and haven't realized their issues yet.

    I see this a lot in esoteric communities because some people tend to be dismissive and gaslighting about energywork or esoteric/spiritual work. Just because it's invisible, it doesn't mean it's ghost-worthy. People can absolutely make corporate-level money in the spiritual community. But the problem is the automatic word associations that people have not unpacked and reframed for themselves. If you don't realize that word associations are so powerful, these are subtle energies that we're walking right into and owning as our reality by identifying with terms. A word or a label is an invocation of its meaning in your life. It may not apply to everyone in every circumstance, but I think you'll find it wildly on point for some people and maybe they will tell you who they are and how much they changed by realizing these labels, unhooking the untrue meanings then outcreating where they were before. My point is not to insult anyone. My aim is to liberate people. If we realize what we're associating with...it can become a glass ceiling preventing us from being able to create the life we've always dreamed of having or preventing us from even dreaming at all...that's where I'm at with this...many people have stopped dreaming.

    If you think the word "spirituality" is woo-woo, does it turn on a feeling or intention of ungrounded and unfocused? Does "being in the flow with the universe" mean not ever choosing and constantly waiting on something "out there" to dictate your success? Are we half expecting people to not prioritize energywork sessions as necessary and valuable? Do we see our spiritual careers as "extra" and not "essential"? Has The Call only landed in our minds but not grounded through our Being?

Do we identify with "boho" or "free spirit" but think that means we have to live a nomadic life and not own our home or that it means we are not prosperous, and automatically living paycheck to paycheck? Do we love boho style but too much of it has become so eclectic it now feels disorganized...more like hobo? What other phrases, labels, and words can you think of that hold undesired meanings invoked and reflected in your world?

My family has always associated me with being the hippie chick of the family, and compared to them, sure. But when I get into some of these hippie communities, I don't. I stand out like a sore thumb. I feel so corporate compared to the group energy present. I am very creative and love the Heaven on Earth concept, harmony and peace as life...but I'm also balanced with analytical and organizational skillsets-I have over 20 years of administrative work experience as well as a highly efficient mind that has reinvented ways of doing business. The common vibe in hippie communities aims to promote light and love and that's great. But while you're promoting light and love, you can also have a business mindset. You *can* have a corporate mindset to the degree that gets you to achieve your goals and set new ones.

If we are going to have more, we need to be more. And we can't be more of ourselves if we don't realize that we're entangled. When your power is entangled outside of you, you can only create limited versions of your goals and dreams. Words have power. They carry energy and they create a force field around us. Sometimes it's not empowering... sometimes it squashes us. I've always said, *"Just because you don't know how you can have something, it doesn't mean that you can't."* The "how" is never your problem anyway. People get hung up on the "how" and they never get started. What they should actually be doing is seeing that they don't need to know the how and knowing that the universe delivers that "how" when it's time, in the steps that it's time to take. What we need to know is "what."

FOCUS ON THE WHAT *NOT* HOW TECHNIQUE

Set your intention to receive the "what" if you haven't realized Your Call yet. Ask the Universe what's required next. **"Make easy and clear the way for this dream to be realized and actualized with ease by me."** As we start focusing on the "what" instead of the how, we call all of our power back to where it belongs- here in the present moment within your body, heart, mind and presence in your aura. With all your power intact, be from this space. Act from this space. Live from this space. Embody this space. This is the space that you were meant to create from. It's all of you.

20

ENVIRONMENTAL IMPACT

After the last few years of so much change happening in our lives personally and globally...the rise of working from home, side gigging...the culture has evolved to basically live in pajamas. Someone coined a fancy term called leisure wear, but basically we've been living in sweat suits, fitness gear, yoga pants, and pajamas. When I think of doing business and thriving as an entrepreneur, what I wear determines how I care. I see myself looking and feeling great dressed up wearing a sexy blazer and jeans, making lists, checking off boxes, showing up for talks and interviews, balancing my day with an outside walk...but feeling accomplished...looking great, feeling amazing. These are things that make me feel good when I think of being successful. If pajamas does that for you, then by all means, go ahead. I'm not throwing shade. There are times when I feel like I need to wear something comfortable because that's what my body's asking for, but too much of that and I personally start feeling like a slob who's going nowhere and accomplishing nothing. Have we noticed how we feel....what makes us feel that way?

I personally would love to see people dress up more and the culture shift out of this slump because leisure wear is nice and all, but it kind of feels like you're living in a yoga world. Everywhere you go, everyone's dressed like they just walked out of a pajama party. And a lot of times, without realizing it, their attitudes match what they're wearing, so they're slouching with their posture and they're bummed. I'm not saying we don't have something to grieve over...be present to your process. But how can we put the past behind us to move forward and outcreate the past, level up from where we are and where we've been without making the extra effort to look and feel different. There's something about a sexy man in a full tailored suit that was made for his body...he doesn't even have to have completely manicured hair. It can be long and flowing or it can be in a ponytail. But if he is wearing that suit, well, whatever style that is that resonates with him...it could be something that's not even trending, but it is his style and it is authentic to who he is. So much sex energy emanates from a man like that. He doesn't even have to make an effort, he can just be in the room and I feel compelled to look his way.

I once sat at a bar next to this man. I really appreciated his eccentric style. He had on the weirdest shoes, socks and a full suit that was so unique, I wondered if he designed it himself. He spiked his white blonde hair up with gel. I don't even think I've seen hair spiked like that since the 90s, but the fact that he was being all of him, 100% his eccentric, weird, unique self...I was all over it (not literally – he was married and I don't do affairs). It was the authenticity buzzing in the room that drew me in and I was like, *"Wow, that's awesome."* It was refreshing to see someone make the effort but also do it in a way that was true to them, not just taking a page out of a magazine. He had his own flair and he worked it well.

What gets you in your zone? What electrifies the air around you in your attire? I mean, for Gary Vaynerchuk, he rocks a tee shirt and jeans. That's his thing. I mean, do you remember him ever being in something else before he went viral, when he started being authentic to himself, hitting his mark, giving advice and hope to people by helping out. His vibe just got bigger and bigger. If you're resonating with something more simplistic like that, your vibe will match it and you'll attract more. It's about tuning into what is truly authentic to you and that's what activates your own self-magnetism. I do resonate with some nice blazers...I love the heck out of them, especially with some dark tight jeans- you can dress that up or down. But if I'm not in the mood to be wearing a blazer, my vibe's going to be off. You have to flow with what you're feeling in the moment and know when you need to lean into feeling better by making yourself wear something nicer or when to relax into *"slouchwear is enough today"*. Be true to you.

What else are we wearing? We wear attitudes. We wear our thoughts and opinions. We wear our points of view. We become what we eat. We wear our environment. There was a short stent early in my art career where family members had to move in and some of them had bad attitudes and negative world outlooks. During that time of overlapping living together, I found that I no longer desired creating artwork anymore because it was tainted by the energy they brought into my vicinity. There was no tuning it out. It was too much to bear. I couldn't create the beautiful artworks that were high vibe and happy, full of vibrant colors anymore...everything just went dark, including the urges to choose dark paint colors. Looking back at it, I see it was spiritual warfare showing up right on time...Right after I received a lot of great press about my art career, then came the emergency of moving these depressed family members into the house. Vibrant colored paintings ceased being created and hues of disdain and fear tainted the canvas instead. My inner world was infiltrated with the energy that they brought into the room and I could not turn the tide.

What is your environment like? Have you had the same furniture arrangement for a decade or more? If nothing else is changing fast enough that I so desire to change, a lot of times I will rearrange furniture in such a way that it feels like I'm in a brand new house. First, I slip into a meditation centered on the goal, the end result for something. In the imagery, I already have that outcome and in that scene, the furniture is moved in that certain new way. In this method, they're tied together in my meditation. It's an excellent way of manifesting desired change because you're tying visual feelings, thoughts, and imagery to a physical furniture rearrangement. Even if you didn't believe in moving physical furniture as a way to help you manifest, you can at least agree that it feels different when you walk in the room. And when you feel different, you feel like something is changing. That something else is changing that you desire changed. It lifts the spirits and renews faith.

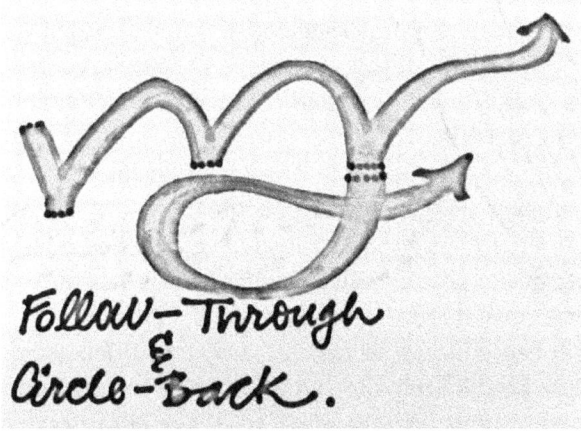

21

The Whole of the Piece that I Am is a Piece of the Whole That We Are

When we take a look at the communities we have, whether online or in person, we see what it took to create them. What we align and agree with and what we resist and react to are often what draws us into these groups to begin with. It is up to us to have a compass, our own North Star ...not to constantly measure by, comparing ourselves to others in an egoic way but to ensure that we are still aligned with our core values, morals and ethics despite what's going on around us.

Values: deeply-held beliefs and principles that individuals or groups consider important. They shape attitudes, behaviors, and decision-making across various aspects of life; i.e.: someone may value honesty, integrity, or family, which influences their choices and interactions.

Morals: refer to societal norms about right and wrong behavior. They are often shaped by cultural, religious, or familial teachings and can vary significantly between different societies. Morals guide individuals in navigating social dynamics and ensuring their actions align with community expectations.

Ethics: the systematic study of moral principles and standards that govern behavior within specific contexts, such as professional or organizational settings. Ethics often involves codified rules and guidelines that dictate acceptable conduct, helping individuals make decisions that consider the consequences of their actions.

The pull can be large, it can .... strong and heavy from a group of people who are like-minded, whether they have all the facts or are making assumptions erroneously....so, it's imperative that we find the group that is aligned with our values, morals and ethics. And if not? Realize the way to stay focused while in the midst of them.

After immersing yourself in a group where things are amiss, will you be too close to see if you begin to slip away from your core Truths?

"The whole of the piece that I AM is a piece of the whole that we are" is a line from one of the first songs I wrote years ago when I learned the baritone ukulele in 2012. Yes, we are a part of the whole but we are whole as we are. And we are a piece of it. So, in order to keep your peace, untainted by the masses who may be misaligned, we must have a focal point that drives us, whether a mission statement, an affirmation, an intention...Spiritual processes keep us focused, living intentionally. If more people lived intentionally, the world would get cleaned up a little faster with ease plus we'd all enjoy the harmony of Divine Order, gratitude, noticing synchronicity naturally and not "on command" to prove a point. When you live intentionally, you realize that life is not as random as it appeared to be because you're setting parameters that are aligned with Divine Order and allowing the Universal Flow to become your priority first.

If our new higher value is Truth and Alignment with the Universal Flow, we have to face the misaligned things in order to move forward. Otherwise, it's like we're putting a Band-Aid on a broken bone while wondering what the stench is. When we are willing to look underneath the Band-Aid, address the true cause of the issue and not only the symptoms of it, then we will begin to heal...personally, nationally, globally, universally.

As we're coming together within, we can't help but notice how much we've grown and how we don't have the same issues and stories we had before. How long did we live in painful realities simply because the stories we told? When we drop the stories and begin to shift our narrative, we realize we can experience something beyond it that's so much greater than we ever thought we could experience...which is great because we've been yearning for more in the first place. Yearning for more, but a part of us not willing to let ourselves go there. Why didn't we let ourselves go there...were we playing the game, blending in with others, not daring to outcreate what has been before, not giving ourselves the space to dream? Were we in the midst of a spiritual battle we had no idea was going on, like having our energy siphoned from us and entangled for other people's benefit, or having our light blown out by dominating forces before we got a chance to start. Whatever the case may be, there's still that little candle within burning bright...saying, *"It's not too late, you're still here. You just need to break through the norm that you've been living."*

As we see that it's our choice to make, and we recognize The Call is still here, yearning to be heard and answered, we know the power is within us to achieve it. We see through the disturbing issues that's developed unchecked over time but are not overwhelmed and dismayed by them...Rather, we are liberated and motivated to make a positive impact...in our own unique way. Whether you've been trying to accomplish something intermittently throughout your life, or your retirement ended up looking vastly different than you dreamed, and social issues weigh heavily on your heart...it's not too late to reinvent your trajectory. Do you now have a new dream? At this point in your life, if things didn't turn out the way you thought they would before, does this new idea give you hope and a feeling of empowerment? As Journey would say… *"Don't Stop Believing...Hold onto that Feeling."* It's your journey.

ABOUT THE AUTHOR

Leah N. Edwards is a visual artist, singer-songwriter, musician, energy healer, Human Resources Professional... and all that is aligned with Divine Order.

AFFILIATE LINK:

Learn Legal Tax Loopholes to keep money instead of paying taxes on it.
Tax Evasion = Illegal; Tax Avoidance = Legal
https://taxrebels.com/free-training-replay?am_id=leahnedwards

MUSIC:

<u>Beautiful Life Unfolding | Leah Nycole</u>

"Beautiful Life Unfolding"
By Leah N. Edwards 2013

Another side of beauty,
Your presence makes me feel.
It's like I know myself better.
Your energy is loving.
Tender & sweet, you are.
It's wrapped in a strong body.
& when I can't look in your eyes
Don't think that I am hiding.
Beautiful Life Unfolding.
Who knew I'd be confiding…
In you-I got a real friend.

I love the way I feel
When I'm with you.
I love how you are real
[with me when I'm with you].

Another day of stillness
Your presence makes me feel.
It's like I listen better.
Your energy is healing.
Patient & kind, you are.
I'm feeling so inspired.
& I don't have to understand
Why we have so much silence.
Beautiful Life Unfolding.
Who knows where we are going.
I'm just happy we are friends.